Ronald Mah

Difficult

Positive Discipline for PreK–3 Classrooms and Beyond

Behavior

in Early Childhood

CORWIN PRESS
A SAGE Publications Company
Thousand Oaks, California

Copyright © 2007 by Corwin Press

All rights reserved. When forms and sample documents are included, their use is authorized only by educators, local school sites, and/or noncommercial or nonprofit entities who have purchased the book. Except for that usage, no part of this book may be reproduced or utilized in any form or by any means, electronic or mechanical, including photocopying, recording, or by any information storage and retrieval system, without permission in writing from the publisher.

Interview with Alfie Kohn, Chapter 9: Brandt, R. (1995, Sept.) Punished by Rewards? A Conversation with Alfie Kohn. *Educational Leadership*. *53*(1), 13. Reprinted by permission. The Association for Supervision and Curriculum Development is a worldwide community of educators advocating sound policies and sharing best practices to achieve the success of each learner. To learn more, visit ASCD at www.ascd.org.

Cartoon concepts and captions by Sonia K. Lee
Cartoon illustrations by David Clark

For information:

Corwin Press
A Sage Publications Company
2455 Teller Road
Thousand Oaks, California 91320
E-mail: order@corwinpress.com

Sage Publications Ltd.
1 Oliver's Yard
55 City Road
London EC1Y 1SP
United Kingdom

Sage Publications India Pvt. Ltd.
B-42, Panchsheel Enclave
Post Box 4109
New Delhi 110 017 India

Printed in the United States of America.

Library of Congress Cataloging-in-Publication Data

Mah, Ronald.
Difficult behavior in early childhood: positive discipline for PreK-3 classrooms and beyond / Ronald Mah.
    p. cm.
Includes bibliographical references and index.
ISBN 1-4129-3714-0 (cloth) — ISBN 1-4129-3715-9 (pbk.)
   1. Behavior modification—United States. 2. Early childhood education—United States. 3. Discipline. I. Title.
LB1060.2.M24 2007
370.15'28—dc22

2006001811

This book is printed on acid-free paper.

06 07 08 09 10   10 9 8 7 6 5 4 3 2 1

Acquisitions Editor:	Stacy Wagner
Project Editor:	Tracy Alpern
Copy Editor:	Carla Freeman
Proofreader:	Olivia Weber
Typesetter:	C&M Digitals (P) Ltd.
Indexer:	Terri Corry
Cover Designer:	Lisa Miller

Contents

Acknowledgments

To my daughters Trisha and Kirstie, proof that good parenting can work! You are the true credentials to support this book. To Kim, wife, partner, coparent, and kindergarten teacher extraordinaire! You are the best. You take on some of the most challenging children and struggle with them with dedication, wisdom, and energy.

To all of the kids, parents, and teachers who challenge me as an educator, therapist, and trainer with your lives, emotions, difficulties, frustrations, and successes. Your stories, more than anything else, are the foundation of this book. Some details have been changed, and some characters and situations are composites of different people and experiences, and everyone in this book has an alias, all to protect their confidentiality. However, each story or example reflects actual classroom, playground, household, and therapeutic experiences.

To all of the teachers and parents who have asked me over the years about their children or about their classrooms or about their families and asked me for a book, here it is!

Publisher's Acknowledgments

Corwin Press would like to thank the following reviewers for their editorial insight and guidance:

Bonnie Adama
First-Grade Teacher
Dorothy Grant Elementary School
Fontana, CA

Alice Atkinson
Associate Professor
Coordinator of Early Childhood and Elementary Education
University of Iowa

Susan Garrison
Principal
Lorton Station Elementary School
Lorton, VA

Gail Hardesty
Early Reading First Mentor
Chicago Public Schools
Chicago, IL

Lynn Hadden
Third-Grade Teacher, NBCT Early Childhood Generalist
Marietta, GA

Steve Hutton
Former Elementary School Principal
Villa Hills, KY

Xiomara Sanchez
Prekindergarten Dual-Language Teacher
Darwin Elementary School
Chicago, IL

Paul G. Young
Executive Director, West After School Center
Past President, National Association of Elementary School Principals
Lancaster, OH

About the Author

**Ronald Mah** is an educator and licensed marriage and family therapist who has worked in early childhood education for 16 years. For 11 years, he owned and operated a child development center. Currently, he is a faculty member of the Western Institute for Social Research in Berkeley, California, and New College of California in San Francisco and serves as a mental health consultant with a number of education organizations and programs, including Head Start, Asian American community programs, severely emotionally disturbed student school partnership programs, and vocational programs for at-risk youth. He also has a private practice as a psychotherapist in Castro Valley.

A former community college instructor and member of the California Kindergarten Association Board of Directors, Ronald combines concepts, principles, and philosophy with practical techniques and guidelines for educators, community workers, and families. He uses humor and stories from his many experiences to help teachers and parents educate and discipline children in developmentally appropriate ways. A happily married man with two young adult daughters, Ronald brings both a personal perspective and professional knowledge to his writings and workshops. He earned his BA from the University of California at Berkeley and his MA from the Western Institute for Social Research.

Introduction

"I have a student—a boy who gets very anxious when new activities are presented . . ."

"There's this really bright girl in my class. She's obviously very capable, but she gets off track so easily . . ."

"I don't understand why last year he was such a good student, but this year . . ."

"My 5-year-old can be the sweetest kid, but recently he's been hitting other kids at school . . ."

"She's an active kid. I could understand that in September, but now . . . just when you'd think she would be more used to the classroom and the rules, she's gotten more difficult."

"She's always been a conscientious student, but it seems like she just doesn't care anymore . . ."

"It's not like he doesn't know it's not okay. He knows he'll get caught. He knows he'll get into trouble, but he does it anyway . . ."

"Timeout just doesn't work for him . . ."

"Timeout just doesn't work for me . . ."

"My daughter is just great once she's comfortable, but she takes so long to get comfortable . . ."

"He's like an unpredictable time bomb—you never know when he's going to go off . . ."

"If she could only keep her hands to herself . . ."

"She's the most disorganized student I've ever had . . ."

"She'll look you right in the eye, and lie . . ."

"There's something about this kid that just doesn't quite make sense. I'm not sure what it is, but I know there's something . . ."

Have you ever found yourself saying one—or more—of those statements or hearing one of them from a parent? If so, then you know what comes next: The Question. "What should I do if . . . ?" Or "What might work in order to change . . . ?" Or most likely, "How can I make that child stop?!" As a former preschool director and current early childhood education consultant and psychotherapist, I hear these questions with some frequency from teachers, parents, and other educators seeking feedback. Their hopes, their expectations, and possibly even their prayers are that I can give them "The Answer" to their problems. If only it were that simple!

The Question usually comes along with information. Sometimes it's short and sweet; other times it is quite involved. Some of the issues are classic child-raising or classroom issues. Some of the behaviors are terrifying. Some of the issues are rooted in cross-cultural conflicts. These concerned folks speak of problematic children, difficult children, challenging children, and the list goes on. The children they're asking about scare us with their behavior. They hurt other children. They make the classroom, playground, or home a chaotic place. They make us feel incompetent. They worry us with their possible futures. We feel their sadness and anxiety. And, either as teachers or parents, we are responsible for their success. Hopefully, we still love and care for them, despite the frustrations. Caring teachers and parents want to help every child to be a "good boy" or a "good girl." Such people ask me about the children they worry about. They want "The Answer."

Whether consulting, presenting, or practicing what I preach, my basic premise is this: If you pay attention to children, you will be better able to understand what motivates their behavior. This is particularly true for children who are unsuccessful in school, home, or neighborhood settings. If an answer does exist, it is that understanding helps us do a better job of guiding and shaping children's behavior in positive ways.

The Real Question

The first question—the correct question to ask—is "What is the cause for this child's behavior?" This book attempts to help educators discipline children properly and appropriately by getting them to observe and know their children before taking action. All children don't act out in the same ways for the same reasons, and so one method of discipline cannot be applied across the board. Of course, some teachers and parents believe their theory works for *every* child in *every* situation. Maybe their method is to put all children who break rules in timeout; maybe a more loving teacher showers rule breakers with unconditional love. The reality is that one size doesn't fit all.

You have picked up this book, and so it's fair to assume that you're looking for something more. This book doesn't offer one answer that will work every time, but it does offer insight into why certain children behave in certain ways, and techniques and strategies for reacting appropriately and effectively to change those behaviors. This book encourages observation of the children playing under your nose, so that your interactions with them will be informed by who they are, not by what they do in the heat of the moment.

Is Your Favorite Theory a Sound Theory?

Do you have a favorite theory that works with children who act out, challenge your authority, or cause some sort of disturbance in class? Do you have evidence that your theory works? What are your experiences with and observations of children who test your limits? If you have a favorite theory that often works, you will find that when you reexamine the evidence or facts, they will support the theory.

From Observation to Theory to Strategy

Sound theories (as opposed to "favorite" theories) come from examining all the relevant information available. Your experience as an educator and your observations of the children in your center or school will help you formulate theories about your responses to their behavior. Let's say you observe that a child behaves better in the mornings than

EXPERIENCES AND OBSERVATIONS lead to THEORIES

in the afternoon—that's data. The data may help you form a theory that the child misbehaves because he or she is tired. Another child who does much better working alone versus working in a small group may lead you to theorize that his or her distractibility is the core issue. Yet another child who remembers one-part instructions but has trouble with two- and three-part instructions may suggest to you a theory of a possible learning disability.

THEORIES lead to STRATEGIES

If your observations and experiences lead you to formulate particular theories, then the theories will also suggest particular strategies. Adults should consider ways to get the tired child more rest during the day. Teachers can look for ways to reduce distraction for the distractible child. Adults need to consider how to give instructions one part at a time to the child who has difficulty in that area.

From Strategy to Intervention

Once we decide on a strategy, the implementation of it is the intervention. If we decide to give a child more rest, the intervention may consist of extending the period of naptime for that child. The distractible child is reached by having him or her work at a corner table that does not face other children. Multiple-part instructions are given to another child on a written list or with visual cues.

STRATEGIES lead to INTERVENTIONS

A Caution Against "Favorite Interventions"

It is important to note that some people, instead of falling in love with a theory, fall in love with a particular intervention. They try to apply it to every situation. What happens when you fall in love with a hammer? Everything looks like a nail. Whack it. Whack that too! A hammer is a perfectly appropriate tool for hammering nails. However, it can be also used to drive screws into wood—though it may split the wood. A hammer can be used to crack open a walnut— but you might have the walnut shell and walnut fly all over the room. You can even use a hammer to turn off the television, but would you? Does it make sense?

All tools are great tools when they are used for what they are designed for. All tools can be used "creatively" with poor to great success. And all tools can be dangerous and harmful if used inappropriately. For some adults, the "hammer" of discipline they love might be restrictions. For others, it might be big hugs. For others, it might be rewards. Most discipline or behavior management tools or techniques can be effective, if used appropriately for the right situation. All discipline and management tools and techniques can be horrible tools, if used inappropriately or arbitrarily. The challenge is to find the right tool for the particular behavior for the particular child.

Your Personal Style—Does It Help or Hurt?

Theories, strategies, and interventions all originate with you. How do you decide the disciplinary action for one child as opposed to another? How do you implement an inter-vention? Your style is determined by your values, personal filters, perspectives, hang-ups, and other issues. For example, due to assumptions about gender, a parent might spank the boys but not the girls. Another teacher may have "bad" children stand facing a wall as punishment because that is how bad behaviors were punished in his or her family. Our experience, our culture, and our habits can occasionally take precedence over logic in determining how we discipline, and we must be aware of and guard against this. If our disciplinary methods are too personally rooted, we not only jeopardize the opportunity to cultivate positive behavior, we risk the chance of scarring children emotionally and psychologically.

> *INTERVENTIONS are moderated by your STYLE*

Results

As you reflect on your personal style and how it affects your obser-vations, the theories you formulate, and the strategies that make up your interventions, you increase your ability to bring about desired results. In looking at results, it's important to keep in mind that there are two kinds: the immediate and the long-term. Immediately, we want to see that boundaries and limits are respected so that every child is safe. For the future, we want to bring about the growth and change of the children in our centers and classrooms.

**OBSERVATIONS → THEORIES → STRATEGIES →
INTERVENTIONS → STYLE → RESULTS**

Answering the Question

The previous paragraphs covered the basics of how to begin to answer those tough questions about behavior that I hear so often and that you probably play over again and again in your head. The following chapters in this book will provide you with the critical pathways in formulating informed, evidence-based solutions.

Realistically speaking, there will always be unexpected and unanticipated situations beyond what any book or training can cover. As a result, this book is a beginning and a wonderful reference tool. Though it doesn't give easy answers, it teaches and suggests ways to go about observing, theorizing, strategizing, intervening, perhaps adjusting your style, and getting results.

Learning and understanding fundamental principles and processes can offer a lot to adults as they support children. You know the old saying: Give someone a fish and that person will eat for the day. Teach someone how to fish, and that person will feed himself or herself forever. This book looks at relevant theories and processes, and how they play out in negative behavior. Remember the **OBSERVATIONS**-to-**RESULTS** process as you read this the book. Don't just look for the "hammer." This book examines goals of discipline, timeout, boundaries, reward/praise versus punishment, behavioral incentive programs, and ways to assess for and deal with underlying issues that may cause more problematic behavior. This will help you ask the questions that will lead to the answers you require.

PART I

The Role
of Discipline

"But, my mom doesn't care if I jump on a chair."

1

Discipline in Classrooms, Families, and Society

It's Monday morning, and Mrs. Jones, the kindergarten teacher, is taking roll. She begins to go down her list by calling out the children's names, one by one:

"Dominic?" *[He's there, in the back of the room]*

"Susie?" *[There she is. . . . little wallflower]*

"Glenn?" *[Present, and cute as usual]*

"Renee?" *[She's there. . . . for now!]*

"Mark? Where's Mark? Is he in the back? No, that's Brian. Is Mark here today? Well, he's not over there. . . . Has anyone seen Mark today? Hmm. I guess . . . I guess he's not here today. He is not present. Mark's not here! Mark is not here! MARK IS NOT HERE! YES! No Mark tantrums! No Mark fights! No Mark arguments! IT'S TIME FOR A CELEBRATION! IT'S GOING TO BE A GREAT DAY TODAY! No Mark interruptions to distract the other kids. No Mark whining to take me away from the others. I'm going be able to get work done today. It's going to be a GREAT day! MARK IS NOT HERE TODAY!"

Which child is it in *your* classroom whose absence causes you to celebrate inside? It's not likely to be the invisible child who never causes any trouble. That child is virtually unknown to you and the other children because she's so quiet. It might be the fidgety one. Or the "Yes, but . . ." kid, as in "Yes, he's bright, but he's so active!" Or "Yes, Carmel is very sweet, but she can't keep her hands or feet still." How do the darlings of mommies and daddies become the good, great, and . . . well, *other* children of preschool, kindergarten, and elementary, middle, and high school? How do they become the academic and social successes or failures of schools and their future communities?

Think for a moment about the opening vignette. Did you laugh? Did you, by any chance, relate? If so, then you've probably wondered how that child became the child who gives you a feeling of elation every time he or she is absent. Is it due to the dynamics of the classroom, the playground, the home, the family, and the neighborhood or the media? The answer is the classic therapist answer: It depends!

Communities That Affect Children's Development

The home, the family, the neighborhood, the class, the playground, and even the media are the communities every child grows up and develops in. Each and every one of these communities influences the child's development and predicts future success or failure in other communities. A young child's future communities include middle and high school, college, various formal and informal teams, performing groups, clubs, partnerships (platonic and romantic, unofficial and legally sanctioned), the workplace, places of spiritual fellowship, family configurations of many kinds, and more. The success or failure of a child cannot be measured in academic or financial success, nor can it be measured by the amount of trophies or other material things accumulated.

> *Success or failure is truly measured by a person's ability to function well in his or her community.*

Home and School: The First and Second Communities

The home is the first community for children. From the behaviors, habits, discipline, and values of the home, they move to the next communities: preschool, kindergarten, and elementary school classrooms and playgrounds. Teachers then face the challenge of integrating the diverse backgrounds and discipline of anywhere from four to thirty or more children in their classrooms, all the while attempting to accomplish the agenda of teaching various academics. Teachers are usually amazingly effective in accomplishing this task—that is, if they can only get the children to sit still, or pay attention, or keep their hands off each other (or out of the fish tank), or whatever incredibly creative, new aggravations children come up with!

Family Expectations and Classroom Expectations

Discipline serves to direct a child toward appropriate behavior. However, the appropriate behavior that is taught in a child's home may or may not match what is considered appropriate behavior in future and other communities, including your classroom. This is often quickly discovered during visits to Grandma's and Grandpa's, where expectations may differ significantly. Or at the grocery store versus at home. Or by many children at the same time on the first day of school. Sometimes the expectations in one's home change with additions or subtractions to the family community. When guests are present, suddenly the dress code changes. Running around in just a diaper or underwear, acceptable and normal at all other times, becomes unacceptable. Or when dad's gone, the food menu changes drastically! The first training ground of socialization—that is, for the child to behave appropriately in society at large—is in the miniature society of the family.

When the socialization expectations of the family are a relative match for the expectations of the later and larger societies, then the child may be prepared for (or at least not surprised by) them. Teachers who encounter families that send successive children into their classrooms find they can predict the fit or misfit between their expectations and the successive siblings' behavior just by reading the class list before school starts. In addition, certain societies or communities (including families) are more or less functional and more or less healthy.

Different Children Come to the Classroom Differently

A child raised in a functional, healthy family may be surprised by a dysfunctional or unhealthy society or community (new family, classroom, workplace, or even larger institution). However, such a child will still be more readily able to survive and maintain functionality and health in the new community. In other words, a relatively healthy, socially and emotionally adept child will tend to do relatively well even in a relatively chaotic classroom with a less-than-organized or experienced teacher.

Children who come with dysfunctional behavioral expectations may be "successful" in a larger matching community but with a continuation of the psychological and emotional destruction they have suffered in their families. Or in a differing yet still dysfunctional and unhealthy community, they may lack a healthy psychological emotional foundation or model to deal with new challenges. Sometimes family members adapt their expectations to accommodate their challenging child, but that child may be able to function only in the family and be left unprepared for the greater community. A family may make accommodations that allow for the child's challenging behavior that few, if any, others in any other community (neighborhood, playground, school, etc.) would be willing to make. This can be a huge challenge for the teacher. Such children enter into the classroom with implicit expectations that the teacher and the other children will accommodate their entitlement, personality, lack of personal space boundaries, fussiness, tantrums, and so forth. Stunned that they are not accommodated, they may respond with withdrawal and/or anger that will compromise the educational mission of the classroom.

> *A family may make accommodations that allow for a child's challenging behavior that few, if any, others in any other community would be willing to make.*

We now return to Mark, the absent child in the opening vignette. This window on his background helps us understand his teacher's reaction.

Mark: Failing in Communities

Mark was a very challenging child at 3 years old. He was very active, very loud, and very impulsive. He was a sweetheart, but (another "Yes, but . . ." kid) his energy and lack of social awareness caused him to antagonize just about everyone outside of his parents. His parents loved him and his 4-year-old brother dearly, of course. They understood his energy and largely accepted it. They made accommodations to help Mark: He was allowed to have more time than his brother to get his clothes on; plenty of warning when there was going to be a transition; few, if any, trips shopping with only one parent; curtailed social activities that would be too difficult for him to handle, and so forth. Their major accommodation was to change their lives and the home community to fit his abilities.

Missing the Point

For the most part, individuals function in communities of one kind or another. In fact, in modern society, most people need to function in several successive if not simultaneous communities in their lifetimes. Mark's family did a "reverse socialization": rather than socializing Mark to their community (the family), they socialized (adapted and changed themselves) to his personality, *despite the fact that his personality caused him to be ostracized or punished by others outside the family.* Respecting individuality must not mean allowing people to express their individuality in ways that are intrusive or destructive of others' safety, sanity, security, and serenity. Respecting a child's personality and individuality is a highly honorable principle. However, in the extreme, it misses out on the need for socialization.

> *Balancing the individual child's needs and personality with community needs and standards is the key challenge.*

From Home to Preschool

As soon as Mark stepped outside of his family, his behavior started drawing severe consequences. In his neighborhood, as much as they liked his brother, most of the other children hated him. His preschool teachers didn't like him, either. He made their lives miserable! He made the staff and the other children feel frustrated and angry. Although the teachers were professional and refrained from labeling him a "bad boy," their body language, facial expressions, and tone of voice clearly communicated their dislike. As much as adults try to make a distinction between the behavior and the child, when the behavior is consistently troublesome and the adults' frustration becomes extreme, then the child becomes the negative behavior and the negative behavior becomes the child.

Of course, Mark's self-esteem plummeted. He had high self-esteem that had developed within his family—his parents loved him! But no one else loved him enough to tolerate his behavior. To them, he was a "bad boy."

From Preschool to Kindergarten

Life became even more difficult for Mark when he entered kindergarten. He had the misfortune of entering a class with a teacher who was "real tired" of working with challenging children but had not yet retired. In her classroom, Mark's behavior was quickly labeled as outrageous and intolerable. The teacher decided that Mark was a "problem child," along with another five of the eleven boys in the class. As the manager of the community, her negativity made Mark's daily misery so overwhelming that he became a kindergarten dropout before the winter break. Mark failed to succeed in three communities (neighborhood, preschool, and kindergarten), mainly because his first community—the home—did not prepare him adequately.

Discipline From the Inside Out

Discipline comes from the inside out in many ways. It comes from the inside, the emotional and psychological history of the adults, and moves out into the developmental challenges of the child. As a former preschool, elementary, and secondary school teacher and now family therapist, I have experienced many children who had significant difficulties dealing with mainstream group expectations once they were outside the family. Oftentimes, their difficulties come from the mismatch between family socialization and the larger-group standards.

Functionally, in families with a smaller ratio of adults to children, parents can get away with discipline that involves intensive supervision and little or no self-management on the part of the children. As a result, children may not be taught or may not be expected to internalize behavioral boundaries. Adults stay vigilant (hypervigilant!) and/or restrictive to prevent their children from crossing any boundaries. They will hold the cup of milk for their children, bathe their children past the time they are developmentally ready to bathe themselves, and intervene with other children for their children when there is a conflict. For a teacher with anywhere from several to thirty or more other children to teach, guide, and stimulate, this intensive monitoring and regulating is impossible.

Discipline Comes From *Disciple*

"Discipline" comes from the word *disciple*, that is, one who learns and conforms to a healthy and positive way of life taught or promoted by a more experienced and wiser individual. Of course, some parents or teachers may not be all that wise despite experience! Often adults try to force their children to make the "right" choices. However, when this backfires, they find they've created highly defiant and acting-out children, or depressed and anxious children who are unable to make their own choices. Discipline in the form of intensive monitoring and regulation may direct more positive behavior, but it does not teach children self-discipline. We can help children make good behavioral choices by helping them develop their self-control, not by controlling them to make the choices we prefer (Gootman, 2001).

Practice Makes *Better*

The Chinese character for *learning* is made up of the words *study* and *practice*. Without practice, study does not create learning. One never gets the experience that promotes and solidifies the learning. Without study, practice does not create learning. One never examines the experiences for positive or negative consequences and a determination of good principles. Practice does not make perfect. However, practice is necessary for learning. And practice includes and accepts mistakes as part of children's learning process of how to have a healthy and successful life and relationships. There will be

> *Teachers need to allow the classroom and playground to be practice places for behavior improvement, and not expect them to be sites of perfect, angelic behavior.*

personality conflicts, stresses, and disappointments in the classroom, just as there are in life. To help children address these issues appropriately, teachers need to understand the children and their own roles in managing them.

Harry Wong (1991) has identified three characteristics of the effective teacher:

1. Has good classroom management skills

2. Teaches for mastery

3. Has positive expectations for student success

Unlucky Mark, from the opening vignette, had a teacher with flaws in two of these areas. Mrs. Jones had poor classroom management skills and negative expectations for Mark's success. Her attitude toward him infected the other children's perceptions of Mark as well. Mark had trouble being successful both as a student and as a friend. The ways in which Mrs. Jones disciplined and guided him affected the way others viewed him, both academically and socially.

Appropriate Discipline Develops Social Competence

Preschool, kindergarten, and elementary school children are fairly matter-of-fact: "If you are nice and treat me nicely, I will like you. If you are not nice and hurt me, I won't like you and I won't play with you." Unfortunately, some children who exhibit acting-out behaviors don't realize the way they affect how other children think of them. When teachers ridicule or punish these children, rather than attempt to help them fit in by developing their "social competence," they perpetuate a developing problem and jeopardize critical socialization among classmates. According to Robert Sylwester (2003),

> Social competence involves the ability to quickly size up and appropriately respond to social situations. Our complex social structure functions via our innate sense of cooperation, early experiences with adults and children, and a set of social rules (or manners) that might actually be quite arbitrary and culture driven. Manners thus don't come naturally but must be taught. Helpful activities are those that encourage the constant informal interactions that allow participants to discover how others respond to their behavior and that specifically teach the social conventions a group must observe if they are to effectively work together. (p. 44)

Most children do not overtly and defiantly deviate from social norms. However, children do not have to be socially deviant, hostile, or disrespectful to be excluded by classmates. Children may only not be in tune to the rhythms of the group or conversant in the social language of peers. Children may be hyperfocused on their own needs, rather than aware of the needs of others. Children and adults who are poorly attuned or poorly socialized to group expectations become socially incompetent or socially inept. They make frequent social blunders and tend to have difficulty fitting in throughout their lives.

Classroom Rules Are Mediated by Culture

Each community and each classroom community has its own sets of expectations, rules, and consequences. These are rarely articulated as clear "do's and don'ts." Harry Wong (1991) noted that "the family as a support group is the guardian and disseminator of culture." Added to the family are schools, communities, and various media influences that all interact in complex ways to create the child's culture. Culture can be defined as the rules, values, and behaviors of a person or group, and children clearly bring their culture into the classroom with them.

Teachers normally set and explain classroom citizenship or community expectations at the beginning of the term: Listen to others, be respectful, do not interrupt someone who is talking, wait for your turn, and so forth. On the other hand, many other expectations are implicitly taught and monitored. Often children figure out these unspoken rules over time only as they break them, fully unaware that there were rules in the first place! In her groundbreaking book *A Framework for Understanding Poverty*, Ruby Payne (1996) made a distinction between gen-

> *Often children figure out the unspoken rules of the classroom only as they break them, fully unaware that there were rules in the first place!*

erational poverty and situational poverty. Generational poverty exists when a family has been in poverty for two or more generations. Situational poverty occurs when there is a death, divorce, illness, or other hardship whereby resources are temporarily reduced. Children from generational poverty have difficulty reading the hidden cues that more mainstream or middle-class children and teachers readily understand. Even if your student population is not from generational poverty, their family cues, rules, and expectations may differ significantly from the school culture.

The "Elevator Rules"

When asked for the "elevator rules," most people give you a bemused look. When encouraged, they tentatively start to propose some rules with a growing realization that they do know the elevator rules:

- Stand facing the elevator door.
- Avoid eye contact, especially after the door closes.
- Don't talk to the other people in the elevator.
- If you must talk to someone, whisper.
- Put your hands either by your sides or in front of you, and never behind your back (you might touch someone!).
- And finally, watch the floor numbers light up as if it is completely fascinating!

How did we all learn the elevator rules? When we were young, curious, and spontaneous, our parents taught us what was and was not okay to do through looks and hushed instructions. Knowing the elevator rules may seem innocuous. However, when someone violates the rules, that person is perceived with anything from bemusement to disdain to annoyance, especially if he or she is an adult. Many other implicit social rules exist:

How late is it appropriate to call someone in the evening?

Is it always necessary to send a thank-you note for a present?

How many times should you offer to pay for someone else?

How many times should you decline before accepting?

Disciplining for Socialization

Discipline can be an effective way to help socialize children to the expectations of peers, teachers, parents, and the greater society. As Marva Collins (1992) wrote, "Remember, school is a microcosm of the real world" (p. 50). The socialization model a teacher presented in last year's classroom is critical to the socialization process in this year's classroom—the current "real world." Your socialization model affects the child's success in next year's classroom—the next "real world," and so on and so forth. When children deviate from a positive socialization model, then discipline may be necessary in developing healthy socialization. Collins continued, "The reason most schools do not work is that school is just the opposite of what is expected of citizens in the real world" (p. 50). As you evaluate your methods of discipline, consider whether or not the rules and expectations of children's families are reflected in your own classroom expectations. Do your classroom rules reflect the rules of the real world?

Do your classroom rules reflect the rules of the real world?

Chapter Highlights

- Discipline is about helping children be successful in their diverse communities: the family, neighborhood, classroom, and larger society.
- If a child misbehaves in the classroom, consider whether or not there might be a mismatch between family and class behavioral expectations.

- Parents may overadapt to their children's personalities, inadvertently hampering their children's social awareness and ability to interact healthily with peers. Teachers may then need to actively promote socialization in their classrooms.
- Children need to be taught about the expectations of the school community. What is accepted in the family may be a major social mistake elsewhere. At the same time, what are understood as social norms by some students may not be recognized as such by others. Clear expectations prepare all students for academic and social success.

PART II

Time and Using Timeout

"Teacher, do you need a timeout?"

2

Before Timeout

Understanding Children's Sense of Time

For young children, there are only two types of time:
"Now" and "Not Now"
Things that *happened before* = Not Now
Things that *will happen later* = Not Now
"Not Now" = "Not Relevant"

What Is Relevant?
NOW and ONLY NOW

Now	Not Now
"This candy is yummy. I want another piece."	"If you eat all that candy, you'll get sick later."
"I love chocolate!"	"Remember you ate too much chocolate cake at Toni's birthday party, and you threw up."
"I wanna keep playing on the playground!"	"If you don't come inside, you won't find out what Chris brought for Show and Tell."
"Give me the paintbrush!"	"Dana's using the paintbrush now. She'll give it to you when she's done."

Children's Sense of Time

Children's developmental sense of time is based on what is immediately relevant in their lives. What is happening now is relevant. What is not happening now might as well not be happening at all. David Elkind (1999) noted,

> Recall memory requires a space-time framework that young children have yet to achieve. It is not until the age of seven or eight that children have a good sense of clock time. A true understanding of calendar time comes even later than that. In the same way, young children only acquire a sense of map and geographical space when they are in the later elementary grades. Without a space/time conception, there is no framework within which to order and store memories. (p. 3)

Without a framework to order and store memories, it is difficult conceptually to remember past experiences and anticipate later consequences. It is hard to find motivation to repeat or avoid desirable or undesirable behaviors and their consequences. Further, as Sylwester (2003) pointed out,

The immediate world is what is most sensorially relevant to a child.

> Our brain oddly has not specific systems to recognize and regulate time, even though we function with a large number of important cycles, rhythms, and sequences, such as those that regulate sleeping and waking, feelings of hunger and satiation, and sex hormone distribution . . . Time is an example of a concept weak in sensory experience that metaphorically borrows meaning from such concepts as space that are rich in sensory experience. (p. 102)

Motivation that is relevant for young children is what serves or disserves them in their immediate situations and immediate present. A more developmentally mature individual is aware that what happened before affects what happens now. In the case of most people, "before" and "now" are eventually integrated in a continuum of understanding about the functioning of the world. Not surprisingly, research has found that attention-deficit-hyperactivity-disordered children and teens have a shortened and inaccurate sense of time (Barkley, Edwards, Laneri, Fletcher, & Metevia, 2001; Barkley, Koplowitz, Anderson, & McMurray, 1997).

How much do you, as an adult, call on the wisdom of experience (what happened before) and the discipline of delayed gratification (what will happen later)? Remember, the wisdom we have now may have been gained from our own impulsivity and errors. Despite our humbling human experiences making mistakes in forgetting the continuum of time and cause and effect, we still tend to be surprised that children often prove to be very human in their indulgence in "the now."

Making Time Relevant to Children

Should adults give up the "before" and the "later" lessons? Lessons about cause and effect? Or about how our present choices affect future occurrences? Absolutely not! Good teaching and positive discipline includes reminding children of prior choices and lessons learned and helping them realize that the consequences of choices extend into the future in predictable and manageable ways. Decisions and choices are package deals that often include both positive and negative results. The decision to eat the chocolate cake is a package deal, which includes the immediate sensual pleasure but also the additional calories, the pimples, the added inches, and especially the guilt!

As teachers teach about choices and consequences, discipline becomes effective when they combine all of the forces at their disposal by

1. reminding children of what happened "before" that may affect their behavior,

2. warning them about what may happen "later," as a result of their behavior, and, most important,

3. establishing immediate motivation and listing immediate consequences for both appropriate and inappropriate behaviors.

For example, a teacher might say, "Jason, calm down. Last time you got into trouble fighting over the crayons. You won't like being on restriction again." Reminding the child of "before" and "later" may be sufficient. It is noteworthy that there is an implicit imperative in the above message: "You better not . . ." rather than explicitly saying out loud, "You may not . . ." or "Stop it!" The implicit imperative is a social communication mechanism to avoid sounding too controlling or demanding, but it is still a command. In other words, this is what you are required to do.

Sometimes an implicit command is not enough. Teachers and parents often encounter children who believe that if something hasn't been explicitly prohibited, it's fair to assume that it's allowed: "But you didn't say I couldn't!" Making a clear and assertive command ("You are not allowed to throw blocks!") removes any ambiguity of your expectations. With the clear command, there is only one consequence that applies now—

> **Commands must be clear and assertive, so children will be sure of your expectations of them.**

your displeasure, disapproval, or disappointment. For some children, and adults, the possibility of disappointment is adequate motivation for them to make an alternate choice. On the other hand, that may not be enough. After all, this is a book about real children and real behavior and real problems with discipline!

Or Else!

When a teacher is desperate to get a child to discontinue a bad behavior or activity, the big guns come out. "Or else" is just such a big gun:

- "Stop it, now! You got in trouble before, and that wasn't any fun. You're going to be very unhappy later if you continue. Stop it *or else* you will be on timeout now!"
- "No throwing blocks. You hurt someone throwing blocks before, and you might hit someone again if you throw the blocks. Do what I tell you *or else* you won't get to [name child's favorite activity] next."

Although these examples include the cause-and-effect dynamics of "before" and "later," they also present an *immediate and highly tangible consequence* to direct the child toward the appropriate choice or behavior—right *now*. Once the immediate consequence is clear, then the child can be gently reminded of how what happened before ("not now") became "now" at a later time and the negative consequences became an immediate reality. *Gently* is the operative word. Such reminders should not be in the form of "I told you so!" While recalling a prior negative event, always acknowledge good choices that have since been made and the positive consequences of those choices:

"You almost couldn't stop arguing the last time we visited the library, but you got yourself to stop and listen nicely. That was good. And, because you were good, you get to go to story time at the library today. Good for you!"

When There Isn't One "Best" Choice

There will be times and situations where it is not a matter of doing or not doing something, or of a good versus a bad choice. One choice may be more beneficial in the long term, while another choice may be immediately satisfying but problematic later. Then it may become a judgment call as to whether you should allow a child to make the "negative" or poor choice. Sometimes it is appropriate to allow a child make a poor choice and experience a negative consequence as a result. Other times, rather than enforcing a negative consequence, you can choose to use it as a learning opportunity for the child to learn about choices. You may give the child another opportunity to learn a lesson without suffering the consequence, but do not rescue him or her or say "never mind" to the consequences. Children can sometimes learn important lessons about choices and consequences from a second chance. In other cases, however, it may be prudent, or even necessary given the situation or a child's personality, to apply the negative consequence. For more on choices, see Chapter 10.

Likability, Validation, Acceptance, and Connection

A discussion of discipline that consists of boundaries followed by consequences seems to imply that children's major motivation is whether or not they get punished. Certainly, there are some "spirited" or "willful" children who seem to respond only to negative consequences. On the other hand, even these so-called difficult children in their "now" worlds are looking for positive guidance from adults.

> *Even "difficult" children in their "now" worlds seek positive guidance from adults.*

Children want the security of stable boundaries and consequences. Children seek to be liked, validated, accepted, and connected *now* with predictable adults. Being liked by family, peers, and teachers happens in the moment and accumulates over many moments. Children want more than to avoid punishment. They want to be disciples! The following is an example of how to communicate consequences and care for children at the same time:

- Name the negative behavior and assert the boundary:

  "Ronnie, remember how mad Suzy was at you when you hit her? You're not being nice when you're mean to her. You won't be allowed to play with others if you keep hitting."

- Follow with validation, acceptance, and connection expressed for positive behavior:

  "You were such a nice boy when you helped her. I think you like to be a good boy who helps. You're a super helper."

If the teacher's validation refers only to behavior in the past, it remains irrelevant. Validation, acceptance, and connection must be offered *now* for the now-oriented child to respond effectively.

Unconditional Love and Conditional Acceptance

Some people may criticize the process just discussed if they believe it implies conditional approval or acceptance of the child only when there is "good" behavior. Every child should feel love without conditions. However, the world is highly conditional in how it perceives children and people. If your neighbor is rude to you, you probably won't have unconditional love for that person. If a store clerk is dismissive of you, then you won't like the clerk—or the store! The real world does not normally have unconditional love for a child. If a child is obnoxious and disruptive in a public place, people do not accept that child. If a child tears a library book, the librarian does not approve of that child's behavior or of that child. The real world, in general, has only conditional *like* (not love!) for children . . . or for that matter, for you or anyone else.

Unconditional love should not be distorted to become unconditional acceptance of any behavior whatsoever. Love children unconditionally and their behavior conditionally. Like, validate, and accept behavior based on the appropriateness of choices. Future negative consequences will punish a child's poor choices. But caring teachers and parents have the patience and willingness to invest the time and energy to teach those "not now" principles and lessons.

When is it a good time to hold a child responsible for choices? When should consequences for those choices take place? To answer these questions, I'll ask one more: When is it a good time to buy property? As anyone interested in real estate knows, now and always now. If it becomes too much trouble for you to battle a child now . . . if you don't want the discomfort of asserting boundaries now . . . if you'd rather "enjoy" a child now . . . then when the "not now" of later arrives and becomes now, turn back to Page 1 and start over!

Chapter Highlights

- Children are motivated most by what serves them best in their immediate situations.
- Good teaching and positive discipline include reminding children of prior choices and lessons learned and helping them realize that the consequences of choices extend into the future in predictable and manageable ways.
- Inform children of immediate and highly tangible consequences to direct them toward appropriate choices or behaviors.
- Always respond to positive behavior with validation, acceptance, and encouragement.

3

Three Common Uses of Timeout and Why They Fail to Work

"Ralph! You hurt Vanessa. There is no hitting here. You sit down here in this chair. You're on timeout! You think about what you did. How would you like it if someone hit you?"

"Ralph! Sit back down! You're not supposed to be playing when you're on timeout. Timeout is not 'fun time.'"

"Ralph! Stop talking to the other kids. They can't play with you when you're on timeout."

"Ralph! Stop singing and making funny faces when you're on timeout. You're on timeout. You're supposed to be . . . you're supposed to be . . . SUFFERING!"

In the previous chapter, I discussed children's sense of time and how it's broken up into two categories: "now" and "not now." This breakdown forms the underlying foundation for a common discipline tool and classroom management strategy: *timeout*. Some believe timeout is a wonderful disciplinary measure, while others find it ineffective. Still others contend that it borders on abusive, especially when timeout lasts in excess of 10 minutes. Perhaps you've heard that an appropriate timeout is equivalent to 1 minute of timeout for every year of age; hence, a 3-year-old can have a 3-minute timeout, while a 10-year-old can have a 10-minute timeout. What is the logic of this formula? Is it logical at all? The confusion comes from there being not one, but *four underlying theories of timeout.* One of the theories, if used effectively, works very well, but the other three can be highly problematic. The three troubling theories will be discussed in this chapter. Keep in mind the contents of the previous chapters, as the effectiveness or appropriateness of timeout is related to how children understand time in terms of "now" and "not now" and how well you understand and apply these principles of time.

Theory 1: The "Suffering" Theory of Timeout

The first theory of timeout asserts that being forced or made to sit away from the other children is terribly upsetting, if not also uncomfortable, for the offending child. The following are some presumptions we tend to make about children in timeout:

1. The child feels punished by the restriction of not being able to play or be freely active in the classroom or other situations.

2. The desire to stop suffering will motivate the child to regret the behavior that led to the timeout in the first place.

3. The suffering is ingrained into the child as an ongoing motivation not to repeat the behavior again.

4. As the child contemplates repeating the negative behavior, the memory of the suffering during timeout initiates a cost-benefit evaluation resulting in a choice to ignore the motivation for the negative behavior or find some other expression of it.

It's truly wishful thinking to believe that young children engage in this evaluative process. Admittedly, timeout can be motivating for some children to change their behavior, if they find the timeout to be a negative experience. For these children, whatever compelled their behavior is not as powerful as the negative motivation to avoid timeout: The suffering works. However, there are children who do not find the suffering sufficiently unpleasant. In fact, sometimes they don't even know that they are supposed to be suffering! Cunning, defiant, and irrational as they can be, they do not "learn their lesson" while on timeout. They may be even having fun as they find creative ways to entertain themselves while on timeout.

Origin of the "Suffering" Approach

It is notable that the foundation of the "suffering" approach is based on a negative view of human motivations. When he looked at productivity in organizations, Douglas McGregor (1960) found two very different sets of assumptions about people: Theory X and Theory Y. Theory X consists of the following beliefs:

1. The average person has an inherent dislike for work and will avoid it if possible.

2. Because of this inherent aversion, most people must be coerced, controlled, directed, or threatened with punishment to get them to put forth adequate effort toward the achievement of goals and objectives.

3. The average person prefers to be directed, wishes to avoid responsibility, has relatively little ambition, and wants security above all.

On the other hand, Theory Y encourages growth and development. McGregor asserts that growth and development depend on the parents' and teachers' skill in discovering how to realize the potential of their children. It is not surprising that many people find timeout negative. If the "work" of school is learning and learning is a negative experience for children, then the suffering theory of timeout seems to be an appropriate approach.

Suffering Theory + Intensification = Potential for Abuse

A child on timeout is supposed to be unhappy or uncomfortable in order for the timeout to be motivating. If the timeout doesn't "work" the way it was intended, an adult may have the tendency to intensify the restrictions of the timeout. A short timeout becomes a long timeout—from a few minutes, to a half hour, to an hour. Sitting on a chair becomes sitting without any body movement allowed whatsoever. Being removed from the rest of the children becomes denial of any interaction with anything or anyone. Sitting becomes standing. Standing becomes the child standing with his or her nose against the wall. Standing becomes the child holding heavy books out at arm's length until his or her shoulders ache! These "extensions" of timeout, as they escalate, can border on abusive.

Unfortunately, these scenarios have developed as frustrated teachers and parents face challenging children who are not motivated by the discomfort or displeasure of a timeout. Or other factors, such as a child's need for power and control, are more motivating than avoiding discomfort. Making the discomfort "worse" becomes a direct downward descent into abusive behavior. Many people have observed and experienced this kind of abusive timeout based on suffering and decided that timeout is inherently abusive.

> **Timeout is not inherently abusive, but, like all tools, it can be used inappropriately and ineffectively.**

Children may or may not suffer when they are in timeout. Even if they suffer, it may not be sufficient to motivate them to change their behavior. The suffering theory of timeout can be a dead end for behavior change and socialization.

Theory 2: The "Think About It" Theory of Timeout

In this chapter's opening vignette, the teacher admonishes Ralph to "Think about what you did!" When Ralph thinks about what he did, he thinks about being on timeout, and, like any intelligent child, he responds as follows:

1. He decides that he doesn't want to be on timeout.

2. He decides further that he will do or say whatever it takes to get off of timeout.

3. He says, "Sorry, sorry, sorry, sorry, I won't do it anymore."

4. He asks, "Can I get up now?"

> **Thinking about it _requires an intellectual sophistication that may be beyond a young child's developmental capacity._**

The teacher told him to think about what he did, but she didn't mean in _that_ way! _Thinking about it_ requires an intellectual sophistication that may be developmentally beyond a young child's capacity (and is, unfortunately, often beyond the capacity of many adults). "Thinking about it" implies that a child can evaluate all the potential ramifications of a behavior—and then logically note both the positive and negative aspects well enough to make a good decision to choose to do the positive behavior. This also involves the ability to note that in the future (that is, a later "not now" time), there will be the consequences of the decision made right now. Remember, as discussed in the previous chapter, if consequences aren't immediate, then they aren't relevant to young children.

In the particular moment, Ralph is angry at Vanessa, and the consequences of his actions are not part of his consciousness. If he could really think about possibly getting in trouble with his parents, losing Vanessa as a play partner, developing a bad reputation among others, and so on, he probably wouldn't have behaved rudely in the first place.

He may be able to parrot appropriate words of remorse and responsibility ("I'm sorry, I won't take any more, I promise"), but these words will serve only to get him off of timeout. They will not reflect true remorse, much less an integration of the issues and the boundaries for future positive choices and behavior.

"Thinking About It" for Cause and Effect and Responsibility

Children do need to think about their actions and how their choices affect present situations and circumstances. However, the command to "think about it" will not automatically make them able to do so. Adults can model the thinking process for the children, who are more likely to pay attention when they don't have a personal punishment to evade. This guidance will help them understand the laws of cause and effect and their responsibility in managing and developing their own lives, opportunities, and rewards.

> *Children need to be guided in how they should think about what they've done.*

Responsibility can be broken down into two words: response and ability. The more ability you have to respond to your world, the more power and control you have over your world. Children need to be taught how to have appropriate power and control in their worlds. People who feel empowered are happier people. People who are disempowered and disenfranchised are depressed, if not also angry and potentially dangerous to others.

However, although helping children think about their actions and choices serves their overall development of character and citizenship, it will not necessarily serve behavior change and socialization in the present.

Theory 3: The "How Would *You* Like It If . . ." Theory of Timeout

When Ralph is asked, "How would *you* like it if someone hit you?" he thinks, quite astutely,

1. "Of course, I would not like it if someone hit me! I'm not stupid!"

2. "But what does that have to do with me hitting Vanessa?"

3. "Vanessa got in my space and touched my stuff."

4. "I like to defend myself from her."

5. "I like to hit stupidhead Vanessa because that's what she gets!"

6. "I like apples better than oranges" (or some other likewise irrelevant feeling).

Children are, after all, children. We may wish that children could identify with other children's sense of distress and injustice and understand that their behavior should change, but if they have not been taught, it's unrealistic to assume that children would come to these conclusions on their own.

Young Children and Empathy

Theory 3 is based on the premise that empathy exists on a sufficiently mature level in young children to motivate change in behavior. Even adults can have low levels of empathy: Consider the millions of viewers who watch TV shows in which people are humiliated for entertainment. Much research exists on children's empathic development and the ways in which empathy can, and should, be developed in children (Barnet & Barnet, 1998; Kohn, 1992, 2000b; Turiel, 1998). However, young children don't have what might be considered mature empathy. For example, in a nursery with several newborn infants, if one baby starts to cry, often all the other babies begin to cry as well. It is as if the baby processes, "That is a very sad sound . . . Hmm? Whatever is going on, I must be sad! Waaaah!" Robert Selman (1973) believes that children don't have a particularly accurate sense of alternate perspectives—that is, what

Young children don't have what might be considered mature empathy.

another person feels or thinks—until the fourth or fifth grade. Even then, children still assume that others interpret situations the same way they do and, as a result, that others will agree with them. The adult version of this might be "I know you don't understand me, because if you did understand me, then you would agree with me."

Teaching Empathy

It is appropriate to direct a child such as Ralph toward the other child's feelings. However, it cannot be assumed that Ralph can readily empathize with the other child's feelings. He will have difficulty complying with the prompt to "Put yourself in her shoes." He will be like Cinderella's stepsisters trying to put on Cinderella's glass slippers—they just won't fit! Young children may be so immersed in their own feelings and needs that they don't even consider the other person's feelings. Or they're afraid to allow for the other person's feelings, because that could mean their own feelings have to be discarded or discounted. This inability to allow for another person's feelings can continue into later childhood, adolescence, and adulthood to severely compromise relationships. The prompt to a child to feel what the other is feeling requires some more specific guidance as to what feelings require attention. "How would you like it if someone hit you?" will serve the development process of empathy if some additional questions and prompts, such as the following, are included:

- Does Vanessa like being hit? (And *tell him* that Vanessa doesn't like it if he does not answer, or if he says he doesn't know.)
- How does it feel to be hit?
- How do you think Vanessa feels to be hit? (And *tell him* that it feels terrible to Vanessa, just as it would feel terrible to him.)
- Do you like things to be taken from you?
- How do you think Vanessa likes having things taken away from her? (Again, *tell him:* She feels the same way he would feel.)

Such questions and prompts are not automatically going to cause Ralph (or any child) to have more empathy. However, they can direct him to the similarity of feelings between the other child and himself. Teach him that there is space for both people's feelings. Prompting a child to feel the other person's feelings also serves the overall development of character and citizenship. However, it may not necessarily serve behavior change and socialization in the present.

Chapter Highlights

- Theories of timeout tend to fail when they assume that children (a) will suffer, (b) have sufficient maturity to independently think about their actions, or (c) have developmentally mature empathy.
- Timeout can become abusive if not understood clearly and inappropriately applied.
- Young children have not yet developed sufficient mental sophistication to reflect on their behavior.
- Empathy can be developed by prompting children to try to understand the feelings of others and then guiding them by suggesting possibilities.

4

The Community Theory of Timeout That Works

Jack:	He took the block away from me!
Hank:	I had it first!
Teacher:	You two take a timeout here and work it out between the two of you. You can't go play until you work it out together.
Jack:	I had that block first!
Hank:	No, I had it first!
	[After 5 minutes of bickering and arguing . . .]
Jack:	OK, I'll give that block to you and I get the shorter blocks.
Hank:	OK. Teacher! We worked it out . . . can we go play?
Teacher:	Sure.
Hank:	Jack won't share the long blocks!
Jack:	Hank took all the short blocks!

Teacher:	Kyle was playing with the blocks too. And, you guys knocked over his structure when you were fighting. You take a timeout here and work it out between the two of you. You can't go play until you work it out together.
Hank:	You took all the blocks . . .
Jack:	I did not! You . . .
	[After 10 minutes of bickering and arguing . . .]
Jack and Hank:	We worked it out! Can we get up and play?
Teacher:	Sure.
Jack and Hank:	No fair! You . . . no, you! I did not! Did too!
Teacher:	I need to get the paints ready for our project. I can't keep stopping because you two can't get along. You two take a timeout here and work it out between the two of you. You can't go play until you work it out together.
Jack and Hank:	Grumble, grumble, bicker, argue, snarl!
	[After more bickering and arguing, Jack and Hank have an epiphany: They aren't playing! They're sitting and arguing. While they sat and argued, each of them lost out. A lightbulb goes on. . . . They'd rather play than sit and argue!]
Jack and Hank:	We worked it out! Can we get up and play?
Teacher:	Sure.

And they went and played.
And Kyle's structure didn't get bumped.
And the teacher was able to teach!

Timeout can be an appropriate intervention by caring adults to build character and promote responsibility and healthy relationships at present and in the future. Timeout, in its many forms, has been a primary avenue of behavior change, modification, and socialization throughout the history of humanity. As evidenced in the example above, timeout doesn't have to involve sending a lone child to a remote corner of the classroom to "think about" bad behavior. Instead, it can be a constructive period in which children know why they're there, know what they have to do to get out, and, oftentimes, must compromise to get what they want.

The basic rule of any community is that individuals are allowed to stay in the community as long as they follow the requirement to *not harm*

- self,
- others, or
- the process or functioning of the community or group.

When a member of a community or a group has become destructive in some way, a boundary is asserted. Such behavior is not acceptable, and the group tends to expel the individual. Churches have excommunicated those who violate the basic rules. Thieves are sent to jail. Those who commit the worst crimes may be put in solitary confinement or even be executed. The theory behind these punishments is the same as that behind time-

Timeout is not an arbitrary process, but an application of the historical community process for survival and continuity.

out: *Timeout is not an arbitrary process, but an application of the historical community process for survival and continuity.* This process, of course, involves removing the offenders from the immediate community, be it the circle at circle time, the classroom, the neighborhood, the state, or the country.

How early should timeout be utilized for children? Early childhood is the best and easiest time to teach toddlers and young children about not harming themselves or others. A baby who crawls around and sticks dangerous things in his or her mouth (harm to self) or abuses the kitty cat (harm to others) is put in a playpen. Baby timeout! In fact, it could even be considered baby prison—the playpen does have bars. Putting a baby in a playpen, however, is not punishment, but protection of both others and the baby from his or her own actions. The baby will not like it and may not be able to developmentally think about it or feel how the cat may feel. Regardless, he or she begins to learn the lesson that freedom to participate in the community requires following its basic rules.

The Three Rules of Community

Harm to Self

The first rule of the community is that you cannot be a part of the community and participate in the community process if you harm yourself. This is critical to later happiness and success. We can use timeout as a way to tell children that they have not behaved appropriately enough to be a part of the community and therefore they are harming themselves. It may be startling for some children to hear that what they've done to another is in fact harming them. This is an important lifelong lesson that is best learned early in life; if not learned early, some people are unable to learn it at all.

Children who are inattentive, disrespectful, and act in harmful ways toward others will experience negative consequences. Other children, teachers, and adults will not like them. Their academic progress will be compromised if they are unable to function in the classroom or with peers. Such children do more than turn others away—they isolate and endanger themselves. They are likely to be shunned and ostracized, becoming vulnerable to low self-esteem, depression, and anxiety. They may be more readily drawn toward dysfunctional, deviant behaviors and peers, and they're also more likely to self-medicate with drugs and alcohol as they grow older (Abraham & Fava, 1999; Grant, 2004; O'Connell, 2005). It is the responsibility of teachers to intervene positively on behalf of these children when they are in our classrooms and in our care, and not simply say a prayer of thanks after we've endured them and they move on to the next grade. A child that is allowed to act inappropriately receives the message that such behavior is acceptable, and that behavior will continue to the detriment of the child and everyone else.

Harm to Others

The second rule of the community is that you cannot be a part of the community if you're causing harm to others. In the classroom, children have needs. All children are involved in a process of emotional, moral, intellectual, and physical development. If a child's behavior is causing harm to the others' learning and growth, their sense of security and safety, or their self-esteem, then that child is a danger to the community. By separating the child, it sends the message that the behavior (and, as a result, the child) will not be allowed in the community. A restraining order is a legally enforced timeout or "stay away" order. Divorce is a permanent timeout. Losing legal or physical custody of children is another painful consequence and application of timeout after continual emotional, psychological, physical, and/or sexual harm to the children by the offending parent. A jail or prison sentence is an enforced timeout of individuals from society who have caused significant harm to others. Why is it that so many people still feel entitled to the freedom to continue in relationships despite the harm they have caused? The most likely answer is that as children, they were not taught proper behavior and respect for others.

The needs and uniqueness of an individual's personality are affirmed and promoted as part of the American educational and cultural ethic. However, an individual is still a part of the community, and his or her behavior affects other people. There needs to be a balance—sometimes a stretch and other times a muting—of personal energy and behavior to respect other people in the classroom.

> *Being part of a community means being responsible to avoid harming other people and being respectful of their needs and issues.*

Harm to the Process of the Community

The third rule of the community is that you cannot be a part of the community and participate in the community process if you harm that process. Each community, be it a classroom, a family, a marriage, or a bus full of passengers, gathers with some intent or to serve some purpose. Some communities are more overtly purposeful, such as a classroom to teach children or passengers trying to reach their destinations. When there is interference with the process of the community, the community will naturally seek to end it.

A child may throw a tantrum, talk or interrupt another child who is trying to speak, steal or break classroom toys or equipment, or scream and fight. These actions either cause direct harm to someone else or draw the teacher away from facilitating the other children's learning. The learning community, as a result, is harmed. Once again, timeout as a consequence later in life will be much more severe than the teaching and developmental process it can be in early childhood. It is then easier to view timeout as a caring and even preventive intervention, both for the child in your class and the adult that the child will become. With this attitude, you'll be more apt to apply timeout correctly, with the goal of behavior change, not suffering.

The Gift of Timeout

That's right! Timeout can be a gift for the long term. It sends a message that certain behaviors will not be tolerated in the present, and this works to prevent a pattern of dysfunctional, negative behavior that could travel with a child forever. Everyone knows of an

> *The appropriate use of timeout sends a message that certain behaviors will not be tolerated in the present, and this works to prevent a pattern of negative behaviors from beginning.*

adult in the family, at work, or in the neighborhood who continues to behave in harmful ways that are off-putting to others. Despite getting into trouble (be it with a spouse, boss, neighbor, or the police), he or she continues with a sense of entitlement. Such people fail to understand that their behavior has caused these negative consequences. They tend to repeat their behavior over and over, unaware that they have violated community boundaries. Eventually, they are forced out of their communities of marriage, work, place of worship, families, and so forth. They remain self-righteousness, but they suffer terribly for decades.

Timeout in the preschool or early elementary school years (or at home) can be a far more nurturing and positively formative intervention than the punishments of later years. Timeout can be used as a teaching tool to guide children toward appropriate social behavior and interactions.

Chapter Highlights

- Timeout can be an appropriate intervention, when applied with care, to build character and promote responsibility.
- Timeout is a useful intervention for preventing self-harm, harm to others, or harm to the functioning of the group or community.
- Effective use of timeout sends a message that certain behaviors will not be tolerated in the present, and this can prevent a cycle of negative behaviors from taking hold.

5

Applying Timeout Effectively

Seth: I'll be good. I won't hit any more. I won't scream. I promise.
Teacher: OK, you can go play.

Not good + Hitting + Screaming = Broken promise → Timeout

Seth: I'll be good. I won't hit any more. I won't scream. I promise.
Teacher: OK, you can go play.

Not good again + Hitting again + Screaming again = Broken promise #2 → Timeout #2

Seth: I'll be good. I won't hit any more. I won't scream. I promise.
Teacher: OK, you can go play. But don't forget your promise!

Not good again + Hitting again + Screaming again = Broken promise #3 → Timeout #3

Seth: I'll be good. I won't hit any more. I won't scream. I promise.
Teacher: You said that last time. You promised that before. You need to have *a new plan* before you can go play. Your promise is not good enough. What are you going to do *differently*? How can I help you?

Begin With Basic Boundaries and Instructions

To assert a boundary, begin by confronting the behavior. This includes naming the behavior and establishing what is inappropriate or appropriate:

> *"Ralph! You hurt Vanessa. There is no hitting here. You sit down here in this chair. You're on timeout!"*

Guide Ralph to think about what happened, the choices he made, and the consequences of his behavior. This is the process that teaches cause and effect and responsibility, but it is not necessarily what will motivate or change behavior. The following are guidance suggestions:

> *"You think about what you did. Something happened that you didn't like, and you hit. I understand that you didn't like that, but you cannot choose to hit."*

> *"Because you hit, you are now on timeout. You don't get to play."*

> *"Only kids who are nice to each other get to play with each other in this class."*

Guide Ralph (or the child in your class who acts suspiciously similar to Ralph!) to think about how his victim's feelings are the same as his. Here, you can direct Ralph so that he can begin the process of developing empathy:

> *"How would you like it if someone hit you?"*

> *"Does Vanessa like being hit? No, she doesn't like being hit."*

> *"How does it feel to be hit? It's not nice, is it? You don't like to be hit either."*

> *"How do you think Vanessa feels being hit? It feels terrible to be hit, the same as it feels terrible to you."*

> *"Do you like things being taken from you? Of course you don't like things being taken from you."*

> *"How do you think Vanessa likes having things taken from her? Vanessa doesn't like things being taken from her, either."*

Remember, however, that children in preschool and the primary grades may be too young, and as a result too egocentric, to truly have empathy at this point.

Continuing with Ralph, the next step is to tell him that you must leave him but that you will be back soon. You need to leave him because, as a teacher, you have the responsibility for the rest of the class and the community process—that's teaching! The break from Ralph gives him some time to think and allows you to refocus on what's happening in the class. After a short period of time, return to Ralph and talk to him about the community:

"Ralph, when you hit kids and aren't nice to them, the other kids will not like you. They won't want to play with you anymore. Do you want everyone to be mad at you? People won't think you are a nice person. If you make other people get mad at you or not like you, you can't be with other kids and you'll be all alone." (harm to self)

"You hurt Vanessa. You cannot hit kids in this class. It is not okay. Vanessa and all the kids need you to be nice. If you cannot be nice to the other kids, you can't be with them. You can't play." (harm to others)

"I have to take time to talk to you about hitting instead of helping the kids learn. Everyone was playing, and when you started hitting, it interrupted their play. You can't be with us if you mess up what we are doing." (harm to the process of the community)

Explain the three rules of the community: that the requirements for inclusion or participation in the community are not harming self, others, or the process of the community. Then check with Ralph to see if he understands and if he agrees to follow these three simple rules. Of course, he will respond that he will be good and not hit any more. He has thought about it. He thinks he wants to get up. He thinks— that is, he knows—that if he promises to be good, you will let him get up NOW! So he promises, and you let him get up.

Return to Timeout

If Ralph is actually able to integrate into his awareness enough of the discipline and teaching, then his behavior will change for the better. Great! However, it is likely that things will not resolve quite so well— at least, not so readily. The NOW of being on timeout has passed and soon will be the forgotten and irrelevant, NOT NOW. Ralph is in a new present—a new NOW. Very shortly . . . bash, boom, bang! Waaah! Ralph has hit somebody else. So what do you do? Put him back on timeout.

Ralph didn't act with empathy. He didn't think about all the consequences of his actions. And whether or not he suffered while he was on timeout before, the basic rules of the community to not harm self, others, or the process of the community should hold firm. Put him back on timeout, and clearly explain your rationale:

> *"Ralph, you're on timeout again because you can't hurt people in our class. You can't play if you are hurting people."*

Again, you come back to talk to him, after giving him a chance to consider what he has done and what he should do instead.

The Forgotten Child on Timeout

Since you are the teacher and need to manage the rest of the classroom, it may be a while before you get back to the acting-out child and discuss feelings and consequences. Realistically, many a teacher has forgotten about the child on timeout because they were so involved in teaching! "Oops! You're still there!" Try not to beat yourself up—of course, you didn't do it on purpose. Your primary duty is to serve the needs of all the children. Being left out of the community and even being forgotten or overlooked is a natural consequence that happens in the real world to people who are "timeouted." When you return to the child in timeout, make sure the conversation you have has a longer-lasting effect than the length of the timeout.

Timeout *Again?*

Ralph keeps hitting. Ralph keeps getting put on timeout. Now, I do not recommend putting a child on timeout for a half hour or an hour, nor have I done this myself. However, there have been children who *kept themselves on timeout* for virtually the entire day. Though their stay in timeout is short, they return again and again because I do not allow them to rejoin the class until they can obey the three rules of the community. That is an absolute! Only when you are clear and firm will a child learn that these rules apply not only to some transitory NOWs, but also to a NOW that is always and forever! In other words, they will never be allowed to be a part of the community if they do not obey these three rules—to not harm oneself, others, or the process of the community.

Timeout in Perspective

An appropriate criticism of timeout is that timeout does not work to change the child's behavior; that is, it does not address the underlying causes or motivations of the negative behaviors. Whatever desire the behavior seeks to satisfy will be frustrated. Subsequently, the behavior often will not change. Addressing the underlying issue involves a more complex process. However, while timeout doesn't necessarily change a child's behavior, it does curtail the detrimental effect of the bad behavior on others and on the functioning of the classroom community. Timeout shuts down the ability and freedom of an acting-out child to harm others. *Focusing only on an individual child's development and growth may be an oppression on the well-being of others in the community process.* Although the misbehaving child does not change behavior in the moment, the lesson, the point, the expectation, and the boundary are asserted that any child engaging in antisocial behavior will not be allowed to be free in the community.

> *Although timeout won't necessarily change a child's behavior, it does curtail the detrimental effect of the bad behavior on others and on the functioning of the classroom. Timeout shuts down an acting-out child's ability and freedom to harm others.*

Consistent reinforcement of class rules may eventually lead to growth and change in individual children. However, "eventually" may mean a long time and much more energy. Other children's learning cannot be put on hold while waiting for "eventually" to finally occur. The other children and the community must not be made to suffer for an individual's immaturity or inappropriate behavior or for an individual's slow or resistant process of change. Sacrificing the other children and the classroom process for an individual who cannot behave appropriately would betray the fundamental mission of a teacher to teach children.

Moving From Timeout to a Plan: Doing Something Differently

Ralph is still causing trouble—are you surprised? You've told him the rules of community, you've helped him understand what it feels like to be hurt and to hurt others. Has it made a difference? With this particular child, it doesn't seem that way. The time has come when you tell Ralph,

"You promised me before that you would play nicely and not hit again. I think you need to make a plan and get some help so you won't get into trouble again. What do you think you should do differently this time?"

The key issue to introduce here is to *do something differently*. The promise to be good is what he did before. However, he didn't do anything else differently. Perhaps he tried harder. However, trying harder didn't work. Something needs to be different in the new and hopefully different NOW. Some children are able to suggest at this point that they not play with or around the child they have had conflicts with before. Others may suggest playing in a certain area away from the areas of high activity and potential problems. If children can give such suggestions, work with them. If they can't, then offer such a suggestion and get them to agree to it. They can't get up until they agree to it. Timeout becomes leverage.

Offer Help and Monitor Activity

The three rules of the community must remain inviolable.

Before you let Ralph go back to the group, add another issue:

"Ralph, you had problems the last couple of times remembering how to play nicely. You hit and got into trouble again. I think you might need some help to remember to play over there. How about I help you and remind you if you start to forget?"

Ralph agrees to this. If he doesn't, he won't be allowed to get up from timeout! Isn't this a great way to "negotiate"? Then you let him get up. You monitor him, and as soon as he gravitates toward the wrong people or the wrong activity or location, you point to him or to the appropriate place. Ralph must obey your direction because he empowered you to give him this guidance as a condition of his release. And if he hits again? Back on timeout. How often do you do this? Forever!

A child who is put on timeout frequently will miss academic opportunities. However, when such a child is acting out severely, it is questionable whether he or she is learning much academically in the first place. Without a doubt, the academic process of the other children and the teacher is harmed by such negative behavior. Timeout is a huge first intervention. It may not "work" to change or extinguish a child's negative behavior. Timeout is not a magical wand that solves all behavior problems. However, it will absolutely "work" to protect others and the process of the community from harm. And it should work to teach a child about appropriate and inappropriate behavior, though this also depends on factors outside of the classroom. So what works to help a child change inappropriate behavior? The first part of the answer to that is clarified in the next chapter.

Chapter Highlights

- When asserting boundaries, clearly name the behavior and establish what is inappropriate or appropriate.
- Explain to children the three rules of the community and the ways their behavior violates those rules.
- Repeatedly place a misbehaving child on timeout—but never for an extended period of time—so it is understood that there is a consequence of the behavior.
- If timeout does not have the desired effect, work with children to come up with a plan to do something differently.

PART III

Setting and Following Through With Boundaries

6

Boundaries

The Foundation for Growth and Change

Block negative behavior = *"You can't play if you hurt people. You are on timeout."*

Assess for motivation = *What need is the behavior meeting for the child?*

Teach new behavior — *"If you want someone to play with you or be your friend, you need to be nice. This is how you ask nicely."*

Child's response = CHANGE

Block Negative Behaviors First

When timeout, boundaries, or motivation don't work, it is not because they are inappropriate. Their "failure" to succeed means that there is another compelling energy causing the child in question to engage in negative behavior. *When this happens, your task is to discover and understand that compelling energy.* It's important to remember that the boundary comes first. You cannot fix a car until you get it into the garage. You won't be able to fix it by chasing it around the block, either. A basic approach to behavior change comes as a 1-2-3 process using the mnemonic "BAT," shown above.

Many people try to start with a combination of assessment and teaching without explicitly blocking the bad behavior. They quickly

A child will not even begin to consider an alternative behavior to replace a habitual negative one until the negative behavior is no longer an option.

determine the underlying motivation and teach a new positive behavior to serve it. However, children tend not to consider the new or alternative behavior because they already have a functioning, self-serving behavior that has history and habit to it.

Habitual Actions Hold Strong

For years, the government and environmentalists tried to lessen traffic congestion and lower pollution from cars crossing the San Francisco/Oakland Bay Bridge by getting commuters to use the ferry system and the local subway, which included a tunnel under the bay. When a part of the bridge collapsed in the 1989 Loma Prieta earthquake, the option of driving across the bridge was eliminated. Commuters turned to the ferry system and subway. Even after the bridge had been repaired, many commuters continued riding the ferry and the subway. At that point, this "new" commuting behavior—which happened to be environmentally friendly—had become habit. Many hadn't even considered it as a possibility until they didn't have any other choice. Likewise, sadly, some parents use excessive corporal punishment that injures or traumatizes, even though it may have no or only marginal effectiveness. When a child protective services report and intervention has been made, such parents are sanctioned and forbidden to spank or hit their children. Only then will some of them consider alternative ways to discipline children.

This is a universal principle that applies to both adults and children: If a bad behavior "works," there's no motivation to change to a more respectful behavior. When it comes to most children, keep in mind that the short-term "now" is the only thing that matters. This is why the first step of blocking the negative behavior is essential. Timeout, which we examined extensively in the previous chapters, is one way to block and prevent the negative behaviors. However, there are times when other interventions to block or prevent behaviors may be necessary. The following helps explain the step-by-step process that determines how far you need to go with boundaries and if you need to go beyond boundaries.

Clarify Boundaries and Consequences

Harry Wong (1991) recommended that teachers assert rules, consequences, and rewards immediately. The setting of boundaries is the foundation of discipline. The first two parts of the BAT process, *blocking* negative behavior and *assessing* for underlying motivations, can be used to anticipate and to prevent negative behaviors.

As a teacher during a summer school session, I and some other teachers did a team-teaching and class exchange process. Each teacher had a specialty and taught it to each of the five classes on different days. At one o'clock each day, I taught art and science to a different class of children: on Monday, with my own kindergartners; on Tuesday, with first graders; on Wednesdays, with second graders; and so forth. It was a potential "perfect storm," as there would likely be some children in each class who would test the boundaries of different teachers in different classrooms. To nip this problem in the bud, I lined up each class of children on the one day of the week they spent with me. Then I told them in the firmest and harshest tones exactly what I expected of them in terms of behavior. I told them exactly the things that they were not supposed to do. I told them, specifically, the negative consequences if they did not behave. And I also told them of the positive consequences of enjoying the classroom and activities I had set up if they did behave. If a child spoke or acted out during this recitation, I would snap back firmly that I was willing to send misbehaving children back to their regular teachers right then and there: "Do you need to go back to Ms. Ono's class right now!?"

Viola Swamp From the Start

I was no Miss Nelson I was trying to channel Viola Swamp! *Miss Nelson Is Missing*, by Harry Allard (1985), is a classic children's book in which a nice but frustrated teacher, Miss Nelson, is overwhelmed by her students' misbehavior. Eventually, she dresses up as her alter ego, the mean substitute teacher, Viola Swamp. The children come to miss and appreciate Miss Nelson after dealing with Viola Swamp. Well, I wasn't too proud to call myself (at least, in my head) Viola Swamp. For 8 weeks, 1 hour each day, I had five different classes rotate through my classroom for art and science. We never had a single discipline issue! The children were virtually perfect in staying within the expectations and behaving wonderfully. Several of them let me know that the time they spent in my class was their favorite time of the week.

I communicated clear expectations to the children in my classes, which included communicating how staying within those boundaries would bring about positive, fun experiences in the classroom. The children knew that yelling, interrupting, making rude comments, throwing things around, failing to clean up, cutting in line, and so forth would get them in trouble and sent out of the room. Taking turns, using respectful language, and respecting the equipment and material permitted them to stay in the room and have fun. With those clarifications, the children were secure and relaxed and, for the most part, had a wonderful experience. Boundaries define what is appropriate and inappropriate, and they let students know what the consequences of their actions will be, both good and bad. In addition, boundaries also define the area, circumstances, and behaviors of safety, security, reward, nurturing, and positive stimulation.

Ambiguity Won't Work

What is the speed limit on the highway? Why, 65 miles per hour, of course. Yes, but what is "really" the speed limit? 70 mph? 75 mph?

Clarity of boundaries and clarity of consequences make life simpler.

And what happens when you go over the speed limit, or the "real" speed limit? Well, you might get a speeding ticket—but you might not! That lack of clarity creates an ambiguity that is uncomfortable and anxiety provoking. Even though I may want to drive faster at times, I wish that the speed limit were 65 mph, absolutely 65 mph, and no faster. It would be easier if people received speeding tickets *every time* they drove over 65 mph. If that were the case, far fewer people would get tickets, and presumably far fewer accidents would occur.

Clarity in Your Class

Have you been clear to your children about your expectations and boundaries? Language such as "You know what I mean" would indicate that you have not stated clearly to the children what you mean. Have you been clear about the consequences of misbehavior as well as the results of positive behavior? If you find yourself making in-the-moment decisions about the consequences (punishments) for misbehavior, then you have not been clear about consequences. If your punishments for the same behavior escalate in severity or if you don't always punish, that too is a lack of clarity. Sometimes positive behavior is rewarded with absolutely nothing—it is ignored. If any of this is true in your classroom, then your task is to examine why or how it is that you have failed to find and express this clarity. If, on the other hand, you have been very clear about boundaries and about consequences, then you need to move on to self-examine for additional issues.

Chapter Highlights

- Boundaries set the foundation of discipline. Boundaries need to be established before there can be the possibility of growth and change.
- Blocking negative behavior is an essential first step.
- Children respond well to clear boundaries and clear consequences. When adults fail to assert consequences clearly, misbehavior persists.
- Adults need to follow through when boundaries are crossed or children will determine that the boundaries are empty threats.
- Failing to follow through is a nonverbal communication of permission to misbehave.

7

Follow-Through and Consistency

Consecutive Behaviors	Effective Set of Responses	Ineffective Set of Responses
1. Swearing at another child	"You're on timeout."	"Stop it!"
2. Swearing at teacher	"You're on timeout."	"You're on timeout."
3. Swearing at book	"You're on timeout."	"Don't do that!"
4. Swearing when hit	"You're on timeout."	[Ignores child]
5. Swearing at pencil	"You're on timeout."	"You're on timeout."
6. Swearing at toy	"You're on timeout."	"That's not nice."
7. Swearing to self	"You're on timeout."	"No free time for you today."

Any single adult response to children's behavior may be experienced in isolation. But what is the *pattern* of a longer set of responses? Effective sets of responses that shape children's behavior over time include both follow-through and consistency. Ineffective sets of responses lack follow-through and/or consistency. Children do not know if the adult is serious when the responses vary significantly from incident to incident. Some children still misbehaved once or twice in my class despite clarity of boundaries and clarity of consequences. When a child misbehaved, I immediately followed through with the consequences I had promised. And most of those children never misbehaved more than once or twice after they received consequences.

In cases where children misbehave despite boundaries, I always go back to the parents or other caregivers and ask about how they do (or don't) follow through with disciplinary action. There can be innumerable reasons why an adult, a parent, or a teacher does not follow through with promised consequences after expressed boundaries have been violated. This may include difficulties with the classroom situation: distractions, inadequate supervision, inadequate support, and so forth. It may also include personal reasons: a tendency to avoid confrontation, a desire to be the good guy, the fear of igniting a tantrum, and so forth. Children normally integrate clear boundaries and clear consequences into their decision making and respond with appropriate behavior.

> *Whatever the reasons for not following through, the key issue here is that the child is not the one messing up!*

Follow Through With Verbal and Nonverbal Messages

Communication is made up of verbal and nonverbal messages. Only when the two components of the communication are in sync does the recipient believe the message to be true. If there is any discrepancy between the two components, *the verbal component of the message is discounted as a lie and the nonverbal communication is experienced as the truth.* Children at very early ages are adept at reading nonverbal cues. Laurel J. Dunn (2004) noted,

> Nonverbal cues may provide clarity or contradiction for a message being sent. If an ironic statement is made with a smile, the receiver knows to find it humorous instead of disconcerting. If we are sending a verbal message intending to deceive and avert our eyes, the receiver knows we may be lying. The ability to interpret nonverbal communication is acquired at a very young age. (p. 1)

What would happen if you were to tell Kendra, your swearing kindergartner, that swearing would be punished by timeout (a verbal message), but then you find your hands full with other children and never put her in timeout (a nonverbal message)? Action and the lack of action are nonverbal messages. You can probably guess: Kendra decides that swearing is okay, or, at the very least, she realizes that she can get away with it sometimes. Take care not to communicate that message! If you find yourself occasionally guilty of this (and who isn't?), figure out why you don't follow through. Is it because you're too busy? Too scared of that foulmouthed child? Too jaded to think anything you do could make a difference? Enable and empower yourself to apply the consequences you articulated earlier. You'll not only respect yourself, but your class will respect you too. Always follow through.

Following Through Continually Proves You Mean Business

Even with immediate follow-through of consequences, a few children will persist with negative behavior. Of these children, some will misbehave several times, but after getting immediate negative consequences each and every time, they are likely to end their misbehavior for the duration of your relationship. Continued and consistent follow-through will help you accomplish this.

Be More Stubborn Than Your Students

Some children are more naturally persistent in asserting their energy. They need to find out whether you and your stated consequences are "for real." In other situations and with other challenges, this is considered not only an admirable trait but also a highly adaptive trait for success. Adults looking for a quick fix may sometimes galvanize themselves enough to follow through once or twice with the hope that it will magically change an obstinate child. The child being more stubborn (or let's say "tenacious," a more positive adjective!) and willful (or "determined," another more positive adjective!) will test beyond the one or two follow-through actions. Prior experience says that the adult has the spine of a jellyfish and the hope of a candle in the wind. The one certainty is that you *will* be tested!

Constantly and Consistently Reinforce Behavior

Classic reinforcement theory states that when an animal (or a person) receives constant reinforcement every time a certain behavior is performed, the behavior is learned very quickly (Skinner, 1938). However, when the constant reinforcement stops, the behavior is abandoned very quickly. Think about yourself and the students who are particularly good at testing your limits. Do you respond to the same behavior in the same way . . . every time? If not, it's likely that you're still dealing with the same child and the same problems! Rick Smith (2004) claimed that he has never seen any teacher be absolutely consistent even with the simple procedure of asking students to raise their hands and be called on before they speak.

When adults apply consequences in the form of intermittent reinforcement, it takes children longer to learn the behavior and longer to unlearn the behavior. There is greater resistance to unlearn or change a learned behavior because intermittent reinforcement has taught that perhaps the next time, there might be a reinforcement. Or perhaps the time after that, there might be a reinforcement. Even when reinforcement is altogether eliminated, however, the behavior may still persist for quite some time because of this expectation. Think about the slot machine, the "one-armed bandit," and how it positively reinforces inconsistently, paying out a few coins once in a while. Even when you're on a losing streak, you can still convince yourself to keep playing just a few more . . . and a few more after that, remembering the handful of dollars that fell out earlier. You tell yourself that this time could be a "payoff." Children who have been reinforced inconsistently by parents or previous teachers will hang in there with repeated behaviors for quite a while, believing that they will be reinforced again eventually. They will test and challenge their teachers over and over again until they are absolutely sure that the professed consequences are genuine. Be consistent from the beginning with appropriate consequences for positive behavior and negative behavior.

Consequences must be consistently applied for the children to learn or unlearn targeted behaviors.

Beyond Boundaries, Consequences, Follow-Through, and Consistency

Only a very few children continue to misbehave after clarity of boundaries and clarity of consequences have been given, with follow-through, and with consistency. For these children, it's important to consult with parents and mental health professionals to look for other educational, developmental, or therapeutic reasons for the negative behavior. Sound ideas and theories are normally confirmed with observable outcomes from predictable interaction. If they don't "work," then you've received another very clear message that your theory may be incomplete, inaccurate, or unsophisticated. Or as Robert Todd Carroll (2005), explained, "Even if a theory is very rich and even if it passes many severe tests, it is always possible that it will fail the next test or some other theory will be proposed that explains things even better" (p. 3). There may be something involved beyond your set of normal experiences. Perhaps the child has experienced or is currently experiencing something beyond what you're aware of. Sometimes this knowledge can lead you to a very simple insight that makes a huge difference. How many children have changed behavior dramatically after someone finally figured out they needed glasses to see the board? However, sometimes it may be more complicated and require additional consultation within and outside of the classroom and school.

No matter the final determination, always work first from a sound foundation and explore the basic principles of behavior. When teachers don't start with rational principles, they can become frustrated and angry very quickly. In fact, anger can block the clarity needed to manage and discipline children appropriately. In Chapter 11, there is further discussion on how unrestrained adult anger harms the discipline process.

Chapter Highlights

- When children do not change behavior although boundaries and expected consequences are clear, it may be because adults do not follow through with the consequences.
- It is critical for adults to always follow through and apply the consequences they say will result from certain actions.
- If children are not responsive to clearly communicated boundaries and consistently enforced consequences, adults may require additional consultation with a specialist within and outside the classroom and school.

PART IV

Punishment, Praise, and Rewards

"I'll trade you five gold stars for one of those big hugs Mrs. Hernandez always gives you."

8

How and Why Punishment Works—And Doesn't Work

Mom: *[Removing note from her son's backpack]* What's this note from your teacher? It says you stole a toy from another child. What is this all about?

Tyler: *[Looking her in the eye]* I wanted the toy.

Mom: Did you know it was not your toy and that it was wrong to take it?

Tyler: Yeah. Just tell me what my punishment is.

Wait a minute. What happened there? It seems that Tyler knew he'd be punished for taking a toy from another child, but he went ahead and did it anyway. His misbehavior flies in the face of a key theory of punishment: the assumption that the underlying motivation for the negative behavior isn't as compelling as the motivation to avoid punishment. Sometimes this assumption is relevant, but other times it isn't. If, for example, the underlying motivation for peeking, touching, or running is minor curiosity or impulse, then the motivation to avoid punishment will often be effective in causing a child to not peek, touch, or run. However, if the underlying motivation is more powerful, then the desire to avoid punishment may not be sufficient to stop the child's negative behavior.

Motivation to Misbehave

Anxiety, fear, depression, loss, peer pressure, anger, and emotional distress can be extremely compelling motivations. In addition, personality, motor-kinesthetic energy, developmental needs, poor classroom management, overstimulation, hunger, illness, and fatigue can also overwhelm the motivation to avoid punishment and cause misbehavior.

Unless these underlying motivations are addressed, misbehavior will continue. Continued punishment can complicate the matter by dividing children against themselves. In many cases, they want to obey an adult and do dread the punishment, but they also cannot deny the other motivations toward the undesirable behavior.

Despite punishment or the threat of punishment, these powerful motivations and urgencies lead children to do things adults wish they didn't do.

Have you ever asked a child "Why do you keep on doing that?" And have you ever gotten the maddening answer "I don't know"? Children aren't willfully making our lives more miserable with this seemingly noncompliant response. In reality, they are often unable to articulate the compelling energy that causes them to behave badly, all the while feeling guilty and ashamed of their inability to be "good." Odds are that many children don't understand why they can't stop themselves, and so their bad behavior continues, and punishments continue, too. Over time, children develop an immunity to punishment.

Immunity to Punishment

"Punishment, another coercive approach, is based on the idea that a student has to be harmed to learn or be hurt in order to be instructed. The truth is that people do best when they feel good about themselves, not when they feel bad" (Marshall, 2003).

Using punishment as the sole approach to discipline children can backfire on adults. As Marvin Marshall (1998) explained, "When students are not afraid, punishment loses its efficacy. Yet, we often resort to punishment as a strategy for motivation" (p. 32). Sometimes adults continue to punish even though the punishment is clearly ineffective, because they are frustrated and they don't know what else to do. The opening vignette introduced

"Tyler." He had experienced many challenges academically and had become increasingly troublesome in school. The more troublesome he became, the more frustrated his parents felt. They tried to motivate him by punishing him whenever he misbehaved in school or at home. After a semester of kindergarten, he'd developed an immunity to punishment.

Intensification and Abusive Behavior

Intensification (the intensifying of what has already been tried) is often the normal reaction to failure. When pushing doesn't work, sometimes pushing harder does. When yelling doesn't work, sometimes yelling louder does. However, when pushing doesn't work and pushing harder doesn't work—usually shoving, kicking, and slamming still won't work. Despite the ineffectiveness of intensification in such cases, many people will continue to intensify more and more. With continued failure, there is continued frustration. This, unfortunately, leads to additional intensification of the same ineffective strategies and interventions.

The real danger of intensification, when it comes to punishment and discipline (as has previously been addressed with timeout), is that it can lead to abusive behavior. In the classroom, intensification might look like the following:

- The loss of recess or free time for one day, then for a week, and then for 2 weeks
- Frequent scolding turning into repeated yelling
- A child not allowed to play with toys being prevented from participating in all classroom activities

Destroying a Child's Spirit

If the principle of punishment intensification goes unchecked, anger can lead not only to abuse but also to the destruction of the spirit of a child. Is it so surprising that some children can't wait to leave their families or that some children come to hate school? When children are punished over and over, their early experiences teach them that adults don't like them or their behavior. Behavior is an extension of energy, temperament, and personality, the natural and necessary urge to explore and experiment in the world. The spirit of curiosity and involvement in the world will be crushed if behavior is not guided toward positive exploration. When children are told over and over that their behavior is wrong, their natural emotional, intellectual, physical, and spiritual energy is invalidated. The role of parents and teachers is to guide children to contribute their unique and wonderful spirit to the classroom, the community, and beyond.

For these reasons, it is indescribably important to have greater clarity about the principles of discipline and the various techniques that may be utilized. As a teacher, you can create a classroom that becomes immune to punishment as punishment becomes your only way to motivate children. More commonly, you will find some children in your classroom have become immune to punishment because of the dynamics that play out in their homes before they come to school. Punishment or negative consequences are appropriate when they are applied with care and with reason. When this happens, punishment can work. By "work," I don't simply mean that the child discontinues behaving negatively. If punishment or any disciplinary technique works, it motivates children's positive behavior, thereby eliminating or at least initially reducing negative behavior.

> *Any appropriate disciplinary technique needs to encourage and validate positive behavior, thereby eliminating, or at least initially reducing, negative behavior.*

Admitting It's Time for a Change

Sometimes teachers or parents with challenging children come to the point where they admit that they have gotten stuck. They say that they realize that what they're doing isn't working. They want suggestions about something different they can do. They may even admit that they now understand that nagging, intimidating, and grinding the children doesn't work—so they ask for a new, improved, and different way to nag, intimidate, and grind the children into better or different behavior! The key, however, is to *do something differently.* Rick Smith (2004) cautioned against teacher isolation. He described a frustrated teacher struggling with a challenging classroom for months, without asking for help. The teacher finally asked Smith for, or at least allowed him to, help, which came in the form of a classroom observation. Smith identified a child with special needs, whose issues and behavior were fairly disruptive. Her needs were beyond the scope of the regular classroom and classroom teacher, leading to her placement in a different situation better suited to help her. The teacher was also better able to serve

> *Oftentimes a fellow educator or other professional can help provide a fresh perspective on a difficult situation.*

the needs of the remaining children. Sometimes help comes from a specialist. Other times getting help may mean referring a child to another professional. Don't you always remind children to get help when they're stuck? You can do that, too!

Discipline Is More Than Punishment Alone

Many people do not distinguish discipline from punishment. The National PTA (1993) discouraged the use of punishment, explaining that "to many people, discipline means punishment. But, actually, to discipline means to teach. Rather than punishment, discipline should be a positive way of helping and guiding children to achieve self-control" (p. 1). The remaining chapters in this section provide you with more information on how to help children change behavior and achieve the self-control that is so important in getting along with others and getting along in life.

Chapter Highlights

- Punishment theory falsely assumes that the desire to avoid punishment will always be greater than the motivation to perform the behavior in question.
- When children are punished repeatedly—while adults ignore other, often more compelling motivation—they can develop an immunity to punishment.
- Adults who become frustrated that their punishments are ineffective are more likely to intensify and, subsequently, become abusive.
- Rather than remain frustrated and possibly destroy a child's spirit, adults whose punishments are ineffective need to seek assistance.

9

The Effective and Judicious Uses of Praise

[In a kindergarten class that's almost over for the day, little Josie scribbles randomly on a piece of paper.]

Mrs. Ramirez: Time to clean up. Put your crayons and papers away.

Josie: *[Picking up her paper and walking over to the teacher]* Teacher, this is for you.

Mrs. Ramirez: *[Looks at the paper, which has random scribbles all over it]* Hmm . . .

Josie: Do you like it?

Mrs. Ramirez: Uh, Josie, thank you. You . . . (really didn't do a good job. But do I say that?)

Surely you've been in Mrs. Ramirez's position before. What would you say—what did you say? Did you too describe a poor piece of work as "nice" or tell the child she did a "good job" to avoid a tantrum or to get her out of the class so you could go home? Or have you ever answered with brutal honesty, saying something like "Actually, it's not very interesting. It's not nearly the quality of art or work you've done before or are capable of." Alfie Kohn has written extensively on the topic of praise and rewards. He has reminded us that praise works, at least initially, because children long for our approval and praise makes approval immediately tangible. Praise must be used carefully, however:

> We have a responsibility not to exploit that dependence for our own convenience. A "Good job!" to reinforce something that makes our lives a little easier can be an example of taking advantage of children's dependence. Kids may also come to feel manipulated by this, even if they can't quite explain why. (Kohn, 2000a, p. 1)

Praise the Person, Not the Behavior

It is important to note that praise should not be praise simply for behavior. If it were offered only for positive behavior, then a child could become dependent on praise or some other sort of positive feedback. When adults fail to praise, they run the risk that a "good" child no longer has the motivation to behave well. In essence, this creates what Kohn (2001) calls "praise junkies": kids who "rely on *our* evaluations, *our* decisions about what's good and bad, rather than learning to form their own judgments" (p. 1).

Without praise as a reward, why should a child continue to make good choices? It is the job of teachers to help children understand the importance of making good choices and how their choices affect them and everyone around them. Once children understand this, they're more likely to behave responsibly both when adults are looking over their shoulders and when they're "on their own" outside of the classroom. According to Curwin and Mendler (1997), neither rewards nor punishments have an influence when no one is watching. Rewards and punishments teach only obedience, while values and consequences teach responsibility.

Praising children's behavior or choices is not the same as praising the character, values, and identity that led to the behavior or choices.

Praise children for being responsible. Praise them for the values that helped them behave in a particular way or make a certain decision.

Pay Attention to the Type of Positive Feedback Given

The following excerpt is from an interview with Alfie Kohn, published in an issue of *Educational Leadership* (Brandt, 1995). It speaks very clearly to the nuances of positive feedback and praise:

Positive feedback that is perceived as information is not in itself destructive and indeed can be quite constructive, educationally speaking. And encouragement—helping people feel acknowledged so that their interest in a task is redoubled—is not a bad thing. But most praise given to children takes the form of a verbal reward, which can have the same destructive impact as other rewards: It feels controlling, it warps the relationship between the adult and the child—and between the child and his or her peers—and it undermines interest in the task itself.

It's not a coincidence that coercive discipline programs rely to a large extent on getting compliance by slathering on praise. A typical example is the elementary school teacher who is taught to say, "I like the way Cecilia is sitting so nice and quiet and ready to work." I have multiple objections to this practice.

First, the teacher hasn't done Cecilia any favors. You can imagine some of the other kids coming up to her after class: "Miss 'nice and quiet' dork!"

Second, the teacher has just turned a learning experience into a quest for triumph. She has introduced competition into the classroom. It's now a contest to see who is the nicest, quietest child—and the rest of you just lost.

Third, this is a fundamentally fraudulent interaction. The teacher is pretending to speak to Cecilia, but she's really using Cecilia to manipulate the behavior of the other people in the room—and that's simply not a nice way to deal with human beings.

Fourth, and possibly most important, I ask you to reflect on what is the most important word in that expression. I believe it's *I*. Even if such a practice "works," it has worked only to get Cecilia and the other people watching to become concerned about what *I* demand, regardless of what reasons I may or may not have for asking her to do something. Cecilia is not helped one iota to reflect on how her experience affects other people in the room or what kind of person she wants to be.

On that point, I like to think about the questions that kids are encouraged to ask in different kinds of classrooms. In one dominated by consequences, kids are led to think, "What do they want me to do, and what will happen to me if I don't do it?" In a reward-oriented classroom, including one that is characterized by praise, kids are led to ask, "What do they want me to do, and what will I get for doing it?" Notice how fundamentally similar those two questions are and how radically different either one is from the questions, "What kind of person do I want to be?" or "What kind of classroom do *we* want to have?" (Kohn, as quoted in Brandt, 1995, pp. 13–15)

Praise or positive feedback can take different forms, while keeping in mind Kohn's admonitions. Here are a few examples of how what you might be saying can be translated into what you should be saying:

- "That is a great drawing" could be "You drew a great picture."
- "Very good job" could be "You did a good job."
- "Sharing your toy was very nice" could be "Sharing your toy was very nice of you."
- "I like a neat desk" could be "You have a neat desk."
- "I appreciate your help" could be "You are such a great helper!"

What is the difference between the first and second sentences in the above series of praises? In addition to avoiding the pronoun *I*, as Kohn (Brandt, 1995) has recommended, by inserting the word *you* into the sentence, *the praise is directed at the person who performs the behavior rather than at the behavior itself.* Without a doubt, positive behavior is appreciated by everyone (especially teachers and parents!) and needs be promoted in children. However, positive behavior is defined differently in different situations and in different

When children are younger, both the behaviors that are considered positive and the commandment to be a positive person ("good boy" or girl) need to be taught to them.

contexts and at different times. When a child defines himself or herself as a "good" person, he or she will find or develop a positive behavior for a given situation, context, and time. Eventually, the *internalized* identity of being a positive person is what determines whether a grown-up person will make positive decisions in life. Fay and Funk (1995) are among many who have recommended making statements of "notice" as opposed to praise, for example,

- "I noticed you like books about sports."
- "I noticed you spent a lot of time on that drawing."

To be noticed is to matter. Attention and the confirming communication can be powerfully validating to anyone, but especially to someone with low self-esteem.

Self-Awareness of Achievement: The True Reward

Marvin Marshall (1998) has noted that acknowledgments, recognition, and validation are more satisfying rewards to children than general praise. Children's sense of accomplishment and satisfaction derives from adults' enthusiastic and profuse appreciation of who they are, not the behaviors they perform or choices they make. Sometimes it is sufficient to notice a child's accomplishment simply by stating it in a way that doesn't evaluate the action at all: "You did it!" (Kohn, 2001). Other times, children can be prompted to feel good about who they are and who they are becoming (a "big boy" or "big girl").

The awareness of this evolution in self becomes the truly rewarding element: "Frieda, you're such a big girl now! Don't you feel good that you can do it yourself? Great job!" From a developmental perspective, it is very important to know what is possible in any given situation, given a child's age and capability. For example, on the subject of toilet training, Frieda should be at the point in her development where it is possible but not necessarily

> *Teachers need to be aware of the developmental appropriateness of the expectations they have for children in the classroom.*

essential for her to become toilet trained. Expectations may vary depending on the developmental stage of individual children. However, there can always be an expectation of good effort and conscientious work—of a good and hard worker. Conversely, praise for little or minimal effort and a lack of conscientious work encourages mediocre work habits and low self-expectations.

Attention, Appreciation, and Material Rewards

It is critical that when a child makes a good or positive choice, he or she consistently receives quality feedback that communicates appreciation. Appreciation and attention are not the same thing, however (Smith, 2004). Burt, a child I worked with, is a perfect example of this notion. Burt often acted out aggressively, but with the extraordinary demands of the new district curriculum requirements, the teacher was inadvertently unaware and unappreciative of Burt's personality, needs, and accomplishments. Burt's

> *Genuine appreciation endures while attention fades, since appreciation addresses the hunger for genuine personal connections.*

acting out demanded that the teacher notice him; it was his way of connecting. When he behaved, he went unnoticed. When he caused trouble or got into a fight, he got negative attention in the form of scolding and punishment. To Burt, however, attention was attention. Once this dynamic was identified, the negative cycle could be broken. If a teacher could find a way to validate both positive and simple acts, the child would no longer have to act out in order to get attention.

While material rewards are often easier to give initially, they're usually less fulfilling in the long run, and most people's pocketbooks generally can't keep it up! In today's world, teachers face tremendous demands brought on by academic standards, and they may feel that they need to do whatever it takes to get their students under control so that learning can take place. But when children receive rewards—or shall we say "bribes"?—in lieu of attention and appreciation (or "loving attention"), they become acclimated to desiring, expecting, and seeking the material rewards. In effect, they decide to take what they can get, material rewards, though they actually prefer what they can't get: parental or teacher attention and appreciation.

> *It takes effort to communicate positive messages and model positive behavior, but it's worth it.*

Praise Internalized Into Self-Praise

Parents often decide to reward a child financially for good grades. The financial reward is symbolic of appreciation. Money becomes financial praise. And it makes things a little bit more fun. This type of reward can be appropriate. However, it falls flat unless there is an ongoing system of appreciation and attention for all the time and effort leading up to the end results. Unfortunately, some parents virtually ignore a child's work and effort over the weeks and months and notice only when a grade is given. If it is a good report card, then there is praise and perhaps a financial reward now; if it is a bad report card, then there is anger and punishment now. The adults failed to nurture, sustain, and maintain children during the entire learning period. If appreciation and attention from adults is internalized, maturing children become more and more self-sufficient, able to give themselves the ongoing praise and support they need in the present and will need in the future. As self-acknowledgment and

> *Ongoing appreciation and attention involves noticing and commenting positively on work ethic and effort throughout the grading period, semester, and school year.*

self-praise develop, adult attention and appreciation become more supplementary. Adult appreciation, then, helps to maintain confidence and self-esteem.

Of course, on a practical level, it is impossible for parents to be present to praise children every time they make positive and productive choices. It is even more impossible for a teacher to do so with the much larger number of children in a classroom. As a result, it becomes even more important for children to be able praise themselves. I used to encourage children to "Give yourself a hug. Pat yourself on the head! Tell yourself, 'Great job! I'm a great kid!'" With big smiles and giggles, they would practice acknowledging what they had done as great kids. As children grow up and as students move on, parents and teachers can do their part by helping them develop an internalized sense of excellence, a good work ethic, and a positive sense of self that will facilitate good decision making in a variety of situations.

Chapter Highlights

- Praise can be effective in supporting and motivating children but can also make children dependent on it.
- Adults need to examine the complex relationship that exists among praise, attention, appreciation, approval, and material rewards and to distinguish between the person and the behavior to best support children.
- Teachers and parents can help children create internalized reward systems, allowing them to praise themselves and develop positive self-esteem.

10

The Most Important Lesson of Choices

Okay, before library, you decide what to do. We're going to go to the library at two o'clock, and you have a lot to do before then. Just make sure you do everything you're supposed to do before library time. You can

a. finish your project first, do your homework next, pick a book to read later, and then play some computer games;

b. do your homework first, finish your project next, do your classroom chores next, and then play a table game;

c. pick a book to read later and do your chores, do your homework next, and then work on your project; or

d. make sure you finish your classroom chores, your homework, and your reading before you have free play.

Each choice is okay with me. You just need to take care of your responsibilities before you start to play. So, what do you want to do?

I choose "e": skip doing classroom chores and have free play now!

Hey! That wasn't one of the choices! You're not allowed to go to the library now.

What? That's not fair!

A Multiple-Choice World

In this multiple-choice world, some children always seem to choose the choice not on the list. As teachers and parents, we offer children reasonable choices that, from our experience, are decent options that respect needs and desires. We encourage children, and often require them, to take care of their responsibilities to the household, to their schoolwork, and to others. However, many children don't see the link between these tasks and their needs. And so, as educator and behavioral specialist Ronald Morrish (n.d.) has pointed out, "We're beginning to realize that children, given freedom of choice, tend to make choices we can't live with" (p. 1). That is, they choose "e." Their focus is often on the here and now of immediate gratification. And who can blame them? We, as adults, often have our own form of choosing "e" despite it not being on the "list" of choices—for example, opting to indulge instead of (a) forgoing that third donut, (b) waiting to buy until there's money in the bank account, or (c) looking for a better price.

Rewarding Children for Meeting Expectations

We want to encourage children to make good instead of negative choices. One way to support them to make positive choices is to let them know of the positive consequences or rewards they can expect as a result of their good choices. Children should experience positive consequences when they meet expectations, not only when they exceed them. Sometimes adults forget to do this. Since the expectation is for a child to make good choices, some people have a philosophy (or take it for granted) that a child should not be rewarded for what is already expected. In working with parents and teachers, a reward system is often suggested to help motivate children to make good choices in their families, school, or lives. A common complaint is that if children receive rewards for doing what they are supposed to do, then they won't do anything unless there is a reward. There is some relevance to this concern, especially with adults who praise or reward profusely. Constant toy, trinket, activity, or money rewards tend to focus the child on the gathering of rewards rather than on the appropriateness of behaviors. On the other hand, teachers or parents can emphasize that positive behaviors are what's

Reward with positive feedback and encouragement, not just toys and trinkets.

important, that the child is being "good," and that his or her positive choices and behaviors are pleasing. Self-satisfaction and fulfillment can lead to positive self-identity.

Material Rewards as Symbols of Appreciation

Material (nonverbal) rewards can be appropriate if they are occasional and clearly presented as symbols of appreciation from adults for the good choices and behaviors of the child. When Wendy was being toilet trained, her parents started to give her M&M candies whenever she used her little potty chair. They quickly realized that making candy the reward could create a problem. They switched over to giving her little stickers that she enjoyed and also praised her enthusiastically for her efforts and success. Each time Wendy used the little potty chair, she got a sticker, which she would put on her kitty poster. Within a very short time, Wendy stopped asking for her sticker rewards. The positive consequence of praise was more important for her than the stickers. More important, the praise directed her to be proud of herself for being a "big girl" who could use the potty herself. Eventually, as her self-satisfaction grew, her parents' praise was unnecessary. The positive consequence of good choices was her growing self-esteem.

Consequences for Poor Choices Are Necessary

Just as good decisions should be rewarded with positive consequences, poor or negative choices bring about negative consequences. Sometimes adults will "forgive" children for their bad behaviors or make excuses for them. However, this "covering" for children subverts or prevents natural negative consequences that should follow. There will always be some mitigating circumstances that might convince us to forgo delivering negative consequences; however, the real world is not forgiving like loving parents or loving teachers. In fact, it is critical that children suffer the consequences of negative choices if they are to be successful in the world.

> *Letting children experience the consequences of negative choices is important in helping them learn about cause and effect and their own power, control, and responsibility in the world.*

As an adult, it is difficult but necessary to tolerate children's disappointment in not getting to go on a field trip because they didn't complete the required tasks to earn the privilege. Letting a child

We should never intend to cause suffering through physical discomfort or public humiliation.

endure the natural consequences of poor choices is important to learning about the realities of the real world. This is not the same as creating artificial punitive and draconian experiences to make a child suffer. Presenting harsh consequences that are extreme and unreasonable relative to the transgression will cause you to lose credibility in the eyes of a child. Children who are harshly punished for minor mistakes don't learn to eliminate the behavior as much as they learn that you or the world is unfair. A sense of injustice can lead to an escalation of bad behavior. Children need to experience reasonable negative consequences as a part of a learning experience managed by nurturing of adults. If they do not learn, they may later suffer negative consequences that are far more unforgiving.

Reasonable and Unreasonable Behaviors

Some children want to make poor choices but still avoid negative consequences and still get positive consequences. That is unreasonable and totally unrealistic. The true choice is between *being reasonable* and *being unreasonable*. Being reasonable involves understanding that good choices normally lead to positive consequences and that poor choices normally lead to negative consequences. Being reasonable also involves accepting the natural consequences of both types of choices.

It is critical to demand of and teach children to be reasonable. The teacher in the vignette at the beginning of this chapter presented four reasonable options. Each option was reasonable because it required the child to fulfill appropriate responsibilities before indulging in recreational activities. By choosing the unoffered option, "e"—to play without having done chores or homework—the child made an unreasonable choice. If children insist on being unreasonable and don't offer reasonable alternatives of their own, then teachers must dole out negative consequences; in other words, they present option "f":

f. Choose from options "a," "b," "c," or "d." Your option "e" is unacceptable. Choose from options "a," "b," "c," or "d"—or use recess to do the chores instead of going outside with the others.

Reflecting on Your Own Choices

Are you a reasonable teacher or parent? A reasonable adult presents a model of reasonable behavior and should be sensitive, attentive, and appreciative of each child. A reasonable adult is consistent. A reasonable adult understands that good choices will normally lead to positive consequences and that poor choices will normally lead to negative consequences—including good or poor choices about supervision and discipline. Do you always make the "right" choices for yourself? If so, do expected consequences affect the decision you make? Are there ever exceptions?

Chapter Highlights

- When given completely free choice, children may make choices that are harmful to them.
- Adults need to ensure that children who make positive choices draw positive consequences and that children who make negative choices draw negative consequences.
- The most important lesson for children to learn is that they cannot choose to be unreasonable, and teachers are responsible for helping children understand what are and are not reasonable behaviors.

11

Motivating Reward Systems

Key Issues and Effective Principles

Maybe if I give something to Lexie, she'll behave better. But if I give her something so she'll do her work, then maybe she won't do anything anymore unless I keep on giving her something. But she's not behaving now, so what's to lose?

Maybe if I put her on timeout, she'll behave better. But when I do that, she gets even angrier and fights with me even more. She doesn't seem to care how many privileges I take away. She just gives me that dirty look and goes and hides her face. And there's no way I can give her a toy like her parents do when she behaves.

Well, I guess I'd be happy if Lexie just tried! She wants more free time. . . . Maybe I can give her some free time right before lunch. She promised that she would "be good" if I let her play. But once she gets what she wants, she probably won't behave or try anyway. "I'll gladly pay you Thursday for a hamburger today." Isn't that what Wimpy used to tell Popeye all the time?

What am I to do?

When confronted with children like Lexie, sometimes it's necessary to set up a more formal and organized reward system. *Reward system,* however, is a term that can put both educators and parents on the defensive. If you've tried a reward system, or parents you know claim that they've tried one, and it hasn't worked, try again. It's true that people often set up reward systems with children and get poor results. Yet among the most basic principles of human behavior is that when people are motivated by potential rewards, they are more likely to change behavior. Even if you do not use a formal behavior incentive plan, if you have successful relationships with children, you almost certainly use an informal, intuitive, and casual behavior incentive plan! And as you read about the principles and practicalities of an effective and successful formal behavior incentive plan, you will almost certainly find that your informal, intuitive, casual interactions and relationships with children follow the same principles.

> *When people are motivated by potential rewards, they are more likely to change their behavior.*

Rewards as a Part of the Process, Not the Total Process

As discussed previously, rewards can be a slippery slope for teachers and parents when dished out thoughtlessly. According to psychiatrist and author William Glasser (1998), adults often use "external control psychology" in the form of bribes or coercion to bring about change in children (or others). But even if the desired change occurs, it's difficult to know whether the adult (and, as a result, the reward) created the change or whether the person chose to change. Anyone can be coerced by rewards into temporary compliance, but internal motivation— that is, when people *want* to change—is more lasting and effective. As a result, it is important to develop internal rather than external motivation. This book's discussion of strategies for developing a behavior incentive plan is not intended to start and stop with rewards. An incentive plan is not a means and an end in and of itself. However, when well executed, such a plan can serve as a critical step in creating the internalized motivation that leads children to make appropriate choices. In the following chapters, many underlying theories of motivation will be examined as practical applications are discussed.

A Reward System Cannot Become a Punishment System

Unfortunately, what most people call a reward system often ends up being a punishment system. Instead of motivating children to behave more appropriately, a poorly designed reward system tends to fail children, and then when they subsequently fail the system, they are punished. The following section discusses some reasons why reward systems go wrong.

Key Issues and the Dilemma

Many people seek greater control in their lives as a means of dealing with the lack of power and control they otherwise feel in their families, schools, and communities. As a teacher or parent, you are reading this book to expand your knowledge, insight, perspective, and set of teaching tools. As a result, you'll have more power and control over your interactions and relationships with children. Children, too, want greater power and control in their lives. Unfortunately, they often attempt to gain power and control in negative ways. When children act out, they tend to receive attention, which gives them a certain power over the adult who desperately wishes to control their behavior. Ironically, these acting-out behaviors are usually attempts to receive validation—not just attention—from adults. For various reasons, the parents or guardians of children who misbehave are often ineffective at giving appropriate validation and attention. Teachers in the classroom may be similarly ineffective. They may lack sufficient skills at nurturing a sense of worth in children, or they may be overwhelmed with stress as they deal with the demands of teaching. They may barely be keeping their own heads above water and can only marginally support the children in their classroom. Punishment usually becomes a frustrated teacher's mode of discipline, despite its ineffectiveness.

Anything that allows someone to gain a sense of greater power and control is highly motivating.

When teachers cannot find ways to validate children, they often end up in power struggles with them, and inevitably lose.

Many behavior incentive plans include both rewards and punishments. Life involves both rewards and punishments. If you already have such a plan, an effective plan that works, then you should maintain it or perhaps only tweak it for improvement. However, if your plan needs more serious reworking, keep reading.

Principles of an Effective Reward System

An effective reward system seeks to accomplish the following:

- Create real (and appropriate) power and control for both children and adults.
- Create opportunities for children to receive validation.
- Defuse the power struggle to create a "win-win" situation.
- Remove punishment and replace it with positive reinforcement.
- Remove conflict and replace it with contracts.
- Remove anger from the relationship.

1. Create Real (and Appropriate) Power and Control for Both Children and Adults

Power and control that is relevant to an adult may not be relevant to a child. As adults (ideally), we tend to think of more future-oriented rewards and consequences than children, who think and experience primarily in the present. A high score on a standardized test is relevant and confirms to a teacher the child's aptitude in some way. It may have tangible consequences, including status, financial rewards, and power or control for the teacher. However, higher scores are not relevant as real power and control for the child. Power and control with children often have to do with having choices. We can always give children choices, and we must structure those choices so that each one is attractive to us.

What matters to children? Sometimes all that is necessary is to ask what is important to them.

Choice Has to Be Real Choice

Sometimes adults present "choices" that are not real. Sometimes the choices haven't been adequately framed. As a result, the child makes a choice that hasn't been anticipated or is reasonable but not the one the adult prefers. Then the adult will say, "Are you sure you want that?" That question is deceptive

Teachers need to present great choices, good choices, mediocre choices, and even "blah" choices and be ready to accept any of them for children to experience power and control.

because it isn't really a question; it's actually a statement that communicates, "That is not the choice I want you to make. Choose again, and make the *right* choice this time." If the adult tries to coerce, "guide," influence, or even intimidate the child into making the "right" choice, then it is not a real choice. The child is not experiencing real power and control. A child "guided" or forced into making a great choice (as the adult sees it) will not experience satisfaction, but will rather learn that his or her judgment is not trustworthy. Let children make their mistakes.

2. Create Opportunities for Children to Receive Validation

If a behavior incentive plan is under consideration, it's likely that the child's behavior has been problematic for some time. The teacher's frustration is typically so great that he or she may not have given validation over a long period. In fact, the teacher may even be on guard constantly, just waiting for the child to misbehave, all the while overlooking any positive behaviors the child may be exhibiting. At the same time, the child probably

> *The beauty of incentive plans is that they can bring about behavior change for adults as well as children.*

expects to be scolded and tends to miss positive reinforcement or validation that may come from the teacher. In effect, a cycle of negativity has been established. One of the goals of a behavior incentive plan is to end this negative dynamic. The plan seeks to give the child concrete opportunities to receive validation and to retrain or restimulate the adult to give validation for structured behaviors. The plan will not work if the adult fails to identify a positive behavior for which a child can receive credit. The adult's acknowledgment (which is critical) of the behavior is in and of itself validating to the child. Most, if not all, recent acknowledgment has been in response to negative behavior. Effective incentive plans break the cycle of negativity by offering positive acknowledgment combined with encouragement.

3. Defuse the Power Struggle and Create a Win-Win Situation

As explained earlier, teachers engaged in establishing appropriate behaviors often get into power struggles with children, who feel continually constrained to stop doing what interests or compels them. When power struggles occur, it is not always necessary to eliminate a negative behavior immediately. Some behavior plans instead focus on increasing positive behavior, moving away from the idea that children must exhibit the desired behavior, or else. If positive behaviors are encouraged and they subsequently increase, the teacher can keep encouraging the good behavior. If positive behaviors do not increase, however, the teacher can say, for example, that he or she is disappointed or regrets the inconsistency of good behavior. This type of focus and these kinds of comments avoid an argument or fight. Fay and Funk (1995) have advised against arguing with children or giving in to a protest; rather, they have advocated that teachers simply state their concerns sincerely and note the consequences, if necessary.

Breaking the "lose-lose" power struggle leads to increasing positive behavior.

The teacher may wish for the child to act more appropriately, but the power struggle is essentially gone because the teacher recognizes that no personal battle has been lost. At this point, the child has the following choices:

- Abstain from any positive behavior (which is normally unlikely), which prevents receiving validation from the teacher.
- Occasionally and slowly earn validation for increasingly good behavior.
- Frequently and consistently earn validation and rewards for behavior change.

The adult wins because the power struggle is defused, and the opportunity for positive guidance presents itself. The child wins because he or she also avoids a power struggle and the opportunity for validation presents itself.

4. Remove Punishment and Replace It With Positive Reinforcement

When focused solely on punishment, discipline becomes entirely negative; it becomes about what not to do and about other "or else!" punishments. Such discipline loses its roots as the way to teach a positive way of life. While punishment and negative reinforcement have been the foundation of discipline for thousands of years, fear, oppression, and exploitation have also been the foundation of societies, classrooms, and families. In today's classrooms, however, we seek to leave intimidation tactics behind in favor of positive reinforcement. By striving to promote the positivity, rather than the elimination of negativity, the energy of our classrooms, playgrounds, and relationships shifts. Critical to this shift is the introduction of positive reinforcement. Eliminating the negative alone is not enough.

5. Remove Conflict and Replace It With Contracts

Conflicts arise when there is the expectation for children to behave a certain way all the time. When children fail to meet expectations, adults tend to get angry and force the desired behavior. As a result, children are likely to be openly or passively defiant, responding to our frustration with the all-too-familiar "You can't make me!" or simply ignoring the demands. When adults counter with "You better do it," the conflict escalates.

> *A viable contract is in place only when the teacher's expectations are clearly expressed and when they are equally clearly understood by the child.*

For the teacher, there is an expectation of performance based on an explicit or implicit contract between him or her and the children. Unfortunately, implicit contracts are often in greater abundance than explicit contracts. On the other hand, when explicit contracts have been established, they tend to be compromised by the teacher's lack of consistency and follow-through—which voids the contract. In saying "You know what I mean," you may not have been explicit enough for the child. Many times, adults are caught in this situation because they are not clear in their own minds. Before establishing a contract, determine the desired results in straightforward language:

"If or when you _____, then _____ will happen."

"If you want _____, you need to do _____."

Make the Reverse Terms of the Contract Explicit

Specifying only the positive terms of the contract fails to prepare teachers and children for what happens when things do not go as planned. For many children, being told what to do in order to get something does not equate with being told what happens when they don't do what is required. For example, some children are told, "If you pick up all of the blocks, you will get an extra 5 minutes of free play tomorrow." Subsequently, many of them pick up the blocks and enjoy the extended free play the next day. However, others don't pick up all of the blocks, but the teacher still allows them the extra time for play! Many indulgent adults don't clearly delineate and follow through with delivering consequences. As a result, they fail to motivate children because everyone ends up profiting, no matter their behavior. The following pairs of statements specify what happens when children do or don't do what is expected:

"If you _____, then you will be able to _____."

"If you **don't** _____, then you **will not** be able to _____."

"If you want _____, you need to do _____."

"**Although** you wanted to _____, since you **felt you didn't need to** do _____, you won't get _____."

When contracts are clear about both the positive and the negative outcomes and positive choices are not forced on the child, then the tendency for conflict occur lowers. As noted earlier, teachers can encourage and direct children toward better choices, but they should not make a child choose one option over another. If a child makes the better choice (the positive behavior), the teacher can respond with excitement and support. On the other hand, if the child makes the poor choice (either the absence of positive behavior or the presence of negative behavior), the teacher can express disappointment in the choice and disappointment that the child will not receive the reward specified in the contractual agreement. Throughout the process, anger should be absent. Teachers are advised to empathize with the child's disappointment without getting caught up in the anger that may result from the denial of a reward. The adult can reinforce the idea that as a result of the poor choice, the negative consequence is disappointing but that a different or better choice next time will bring about the contractual reward.

6. Remove Anger From the Relationship

Teachers need to be vigilant in preventing themselves from getting angry, and recognize that children are quick to anger. When children are denied rewards and become angry, they will have difficulty taking responsibility for their choices and learning the lesson at hand. By remaining calm, you can reiterate the importance of learning from a poor choice and making a better choice next time. If you become too angry, the child's attention will be drawn to that anger and away from a learning opportunity. Sometimes what we intend to say comes out poorly or inappropriately. Our intentions get confused, and children have confusion and difficulty figuring out how to deal with us. Jim Fay and David Funk (1995) have stated the importance of adults providing limits in a caring way. Adults need to stay calm and avoid provoking, threatening, moralizing, or lecturing. Unfortunately, adults can become frustrated and confused themselves, leading to the loss of compassion and the eruption of anger.

Sometimes the message that comes from teachers is primarily that they are angry. And that it is the child's fault. And that the child must do something so that the teacher is no longer angry. The anger normally comes out of the frustration of the teacher. Anger can become counterproductive to the effectiveness of an incentive plan and of any discipline. This is a functional perspective, not a moral perspective, about anger. Adult anger may be normal and appropriate, but when it is too intense, it will defeat the

> *Anger can become counter-productive to the effectiveness of an incentive plan and of any discipline.*

learning—the result of discipline that is intended. When the anger is too intense, it becomes terrifying to a child. Rick Smith (2004) distinguished the normal process of anger to reactivity, which "is a choice that we make to take our anger out on someone." When the anger is too intense, it draws virtually the entire attention of the child to the anger. Whatever lessons were intended to be taught, whatever you wanted the child to learn, the opportunity to teach . . . all are lost as the child's focus is drawn to the anger and to avoiding the anger. Instead, the child learns to never get or allow his or her teacher or parents to get mad. Or the child learns that it is his or her fault that the adult is angry or that personal needs must be subjugated to keep the adult happy or pleased. Or the child learns that he or she is helpless in feeling terror, facing the rage of the adult authority figure. Or the child learns that the adult hates him or her. A well-designed incentive plan helps keep adult anger from getting out of hand—and keeps children more connected to the discipline.

Chapter Highlights

- Power and control boundaries need to be addressed in creating a realistic reward system.
- A good reward system restores an appropriate and effective validation process to adults and children who have forgotten how to give and receive validation.
- The dysfunctional and mutually punishing cycle of power struggles is broken in a good reward system.

- It's critical to create real power, control, and choice for children.
- Positive reinforcement should replace punishment in an effective behavior incentive plan.
- When the anger is too intense, it draws virtually the entire attention of the child to the anger.

12

Rewards-Only Behavior Plans

Desirée had been successfully following through and earning points throughout the week. She was excited and looking forward to "cashing in" her points for time to play a game on the classroom computer. Late in the week, however, she got into a fight with Danny after he took a glue stick away from her.

The teacher, upset with Desirée, wiped all her points off of the ledger. Despite the fact that she'd been behaving with regard to the issues they'd agreed upon (morning routine transitions), the girl was denied her reward.

In response, Desirée stopped trying altogether, thinking, "Forget it! I quit! There's no point. Teacher will always make up some excuse and I won't get a reward . . . ever!"

Who really messed up? Not Desirée.

There are many well-designed incentive programs (for example, *Big Bucks: A Creative Discipline System*, developed by Carolyn Thompson Pruitt and Joanna Lebo, 1998, of the Hazelwood Reidsville City School) that include both earning and losing rewards ("money") for positive or negative behavior. However, in certain cases, behavior incentive plans don't work when they outline conditions for both rewards and punishments. Some children come to the classroom with an immunity to punishment. For other children, "reasonable" negative consequences might be too sensational if they are hypersensitive from punishments dispensed on them over the years. In such situations, it's wise to make the behavior incentive plan *rewards-only*. In addition, a rewards-only approach tends to promote a more positive atmosphere in the classroom.

"Rewards-Only" Means Just That

When you start out with a rewards-only plan, determine that you will never penalize children by removing already-earned rewards or punish out of desperation to regain control. Removing already-gained rewards or "points" serves to discourage children from trying. The removal of rewards or points is symbolically (if not also functionally) the same as a punishment. This type of response can result in an escalating cycle of frustration, leading to harmful behavior.

Unfortunately, teachers sometimes remove rewards or points in response to an unexpected transgression—one not discussed or included in the behavior incentive plan.

From the child's perspective, everything he or she has earned and has been working at for weeks disappears in an instant. Everything gained for previous good behavior now counts for nothing as a result of one mistake. In such an arbitrary and unfair world, what's the point? Point removal is one of the primary ways in which adults sabotage a behavior incentive plan. This is where plans tend to go wrong—the instinct to punish for some adults is that strong.

To treat children fairly, in the same sort of way the world will treat them, we must honor their accomplishments rather than dismiss them. In the adult world, if you make a big mistake at work, you may indeed be fired. However, you are entitled to payment for the hours you had worked up until the moment you're fired. No employer would, or could, legally say, "Never mind your pay, you don't deserve it anymore!"

Always keep in mind that children can—and will—test your limits. As their frustration increases, you can stabilize the situation by recognizing their escalating stages of frustration (Fitzsimmons, 1998) and responding appropriately, without punishing.

Stage	Child Behavior	Teacher Response
Anxiety	Student sighs or uses other nonverbal cues.	Use active listening and nonjudgmental talk.
Stress	Minor behavior problems	Use proximity control, boost student interest in the learning, or provide assistance with assignments.
Defensiveness	Arguing and complaining	Remind student of rules. Employ conflict resolution strategies and encourage the child to ask for help.
Physical aggression	Hitting, biting, kicking, object throwing	Escort the child from class, get help, restrain child (if necessary), and protect the safety of other children.
Tension reduction	Crying, verbal venting, becoming sullen and withdrawn	Use supportive or punishment techniques to help the child gain insight into feelings and behavior.

SOURCE: ERIC Clearinghouse on Disabilities and Gifted Education. Copyright ©1998.

Basic Terms of the Plan

Suppose a child is particularly disruptive during the morning routines in your class. A rewards-only plan may be completely applicable to a child like Desirée, of the opening vignette, who has issues organizing herself to transition into other activities. For each element successfully carried out (sitting in the circle by a certain time, washing up, gathering work material, and preparing to leave), the child should gain one or more points. Once a certain number of points have been accumulated, the child exchanges them for a predetermined reward, such as extra computer time, a treat, free play time, stickers, and so forth.

Have Realistic Expectations

The teacher should not expect that Desirée will behave perfectly just because of a behavior incentive plan. There is not only a likelihood that she will make a mistake but actually a high probability. Expect it! For the most part, behavior incentive plans work, but it takes time to bring about significant change.

Make the Plan Practical

A behavior incentive plan has to be specific and practical. It cannot be a plan that requires the child to go from difficult to darling. It cannot be a plan that addresses any and all behaviors you want to eliminate. It's important to remember that a pattern of negative behavior that resists informal discipline has developed over a long period of time. It is impractical to think and hope that the behavior incentive plan, no matter how well designed it is, will turn everything around. Start simple, make it work, and then build from there.

Rather than being all-inclusive, a behavior incentive plan is a beginning step in an overall plan and process to turn the child's behavior in the right direction.

Focus on One Aspect of Behavior at a Time

It is critical to focus on a particular, relatively confined, and concrete area of classroom behavior.

Specific and Concrete	General and Too Broad
Keep your desk clear of papers.	Be a "good girl."
Put your things away when you leave the center.	Play nicely with other children.

Once one particular area has been stabilized—the behavior has evolved to a more tolerable or acceptable level—then another area can be chosen. Or perhaps the first area can be expanded. Some people are not satisfied with this approach, since it appears to be working on areas that are relatively minor. They want bigger change in more substantial areas. But if a teacher is considering a behavior incentive plan, the broad overall change is likely too great a challenge to be tackled initially. Breaking difficult behaviors down into simpler, individual elements creates the foundation for a more effective plan and for handling more complex behaviors over time.

Substantial change may be unrealistic at the beginning. Unrealistic initial expectations serve to set up everyone for failure by asking for too much, too soon.

Start With Short Time Frames and Increase as Appropriate

For young children, plans should be simple and have a short time frame: a half day, 1 day, 2 days, up to a week or 2 weeks. Longer goals of a month, 3 months, or 6 months could be inappropriate for them, as you may recall from the concepts of "now" and "not now" discussed in Chapter 2.

For preschoolers and early elementary students, the day may need to be broken up into several "periods." Each of the following could constitute one period:

- The transition from being dropped off to the beginning of class
- From the "morning hello" and activities until the first recess or break
- The first recess
- The period after the first recess
- Lunchtime
- The period after lunch
- Afternoon recess
- The period after the afternoon recess
- The cleanup and going-home transition

A period could be as short as an hour of positive behavior. The next level of evaluation (or set of behaviors) would be the half day or the full day. Then 2 or 3 days may be the third level, and a whole week would be the fourth level. Depending on the challenges faced, teachers may give *themselves* a reward if a difficult child gets through a whole solid day successfully! As everyone knows, if the children had a great week, the teacher had a great week, too.

Success in One Area of Behavior Transfers to Other Areas

A fascinating dynamic occurs when a "simple" behavior plan succeeds. Having an experience of success often *breaks the relentless cycle of negativity and failure* that had come to define the adult-child relationship. All six principles discussed earlier are activated:

1. Power and control are created for both children and teachers or parents.

2. A means is created for the child to receive validation.

3. The power struggle has been defused, and a "win-win" situation has been created.

4. Punishment has been removed and been replaced with reinforcement/reward principles.

5. Conflict is removed and is replaced with contracts.

6. Everyone is happier and not angry.

Positive energy and a sense of accomplishment give the child a more positive outlook and typically lead to more respectful behavior, even though these areas might not have been addressed specifically in the behavior plan. In one school, a child had been having problems using the restroom without getting very distracted and taking too long. A behavior incentive plan motivated him to use the restroom appropriately, in a timely fashion, and without making a mess. When he succeeded, he felt quite proud of himself. The teacher was able to use that success as a springboard to making other adjustments in his behavior. Another child who had become successful in keeping her desk neat began to take pride in doing neat work. These are small successes, but remember, many children with problems had no successes whatsoever over extended periods of time, and their teachers had little or no successes with them previously, either.

> *With small successes, adults and children see hope and investment rewarded. As a result, they are more likely to reinvest hope and energy.*

Chapter Highlights

- When ineffective punishments dominate the discipline process, a rewards-only behavior incentive plan may be the best option for positive change.
- Resist the old instinct to punish a child for misbehavior by erasing points earned, which sabotages the plan.
- Make incentive plans specific, simple, and practical. Focus initially on one particular relatively confined and concrete area of behavior.
- Success in one area will transfer to other areas.

13

Connecting Goals to Motivating Rewards

Dad: Okay, this reward plan sounds like it might work.

Pablo: Okay.

Dad: The goals I want you to work on are picking up your toys, doing your daily reading, and getting everything into your backpack before we leave for school in the morning.

Pablo: Okay. And you and the teacher said I can get rewards. I like . . .

Dad: Books! Books would be great.

Pablo: I want . . .

Dad: There are a lot of good educational books.

Pablo: But I don't want books.

Dad: Books are good for you.

Pablo: But I like "Magic" cards.

Dad: Books are better for you.

Pablo: I changed my mind. I don't a reward plan.

A critical step in creating a practical behavior incentive plan is the careful selection of *appropriate goals* and the *subsequent rewards.* Goals need to be age-appropriate and relevant to the situation. Goals should not be too far-fetched. The goal of getting into a good college is not an appropriate goal for a kindergartner! Rewards also should not be too elaborate or far-fetched. A contribution to the child's college fund is not motivating for a second grader! Appropriate goals and motivating rewards are part of a specific and practical plan. Successful casual and intuitive plans normally have developmentally and otherwise appropriate goals and individually motivating rewards for the targeted children.

Defining Goals and Rewards

Goals and rewards are different but related. *Goals* are defined by adults as accomplishments that are productive in both the short term and the long term. Short-term goals may serve to increase the functionality of the classroom or household routines. They help reduce conflict and increase cooperation—fewer hassles and fewer fights! Longer-term goals develop attitudes, values, and behaviors that will have positive consequences in the child's personality and life. For example, a strong work ethic is a positive long-term goal.

When children define goals, they tend to be focused on very short-term issues, for example, staying out of trouble or getting something they want (a toy or being allowed to play). It is up to adults to take the lead and assert the value of goals that have a more enduring positive benefit for children. In that sense, goals reflect the values and morals of the communities children will be a part of for the rest of their lives. Putting toys away serves current functional needs that children understand (organization, being able to find them later, and so forth), but it is also related to and representative of responsibility to self and others. On the other hand, verbally drilling young children on the importance of mature behaviors may get nods from them, but they often do not take away real learning or internalize the principles because the relevance is not immediately clear.

Goals need to reflect the expectations and standards of society for its citizens.

Well-designed simple behavior goals learned in conjunction with subsequent behavioral goals will eventually create mature, responsible adults.

Set Goals With Children's Input

Teachers must choose and decide on the goals, but it is essential to involve children in these decisions. For example, behaviors that make up the morning routine, behaviors that facilitate the transition from the classroom to the playground, behaviors involving chores, classroom routines, homework, and so forth are goals that might be chosen by adults. It is important to choose goals that children are at least somewhat willing to try for and that have relevance to them.

Choosing Quantifiable Goals

Make sure that goals are objectively quantifiable. If there is a subjective judgment as to whether or not a goal has been achieved, then it is not quantifiable. It should be obvious and clear to both the adult and the child whether or not a goal has been achieved. This frees the adult from making a judgment call that the child may not respect—or worse, not understand. Specifying that children should be "better," "faster," or "neater" with regard to a particular task is too subjective. On the other hand, goals can also be too absolute and not take into account positive aspects of the child's behavior. Children could be "good" all day long according to the definitions in the contract but then misbehave in the last half hour before parents come to pick them up. If this one act disqualifies them from achieving the goal, then the goal is too narrow.

The Difficulty With "Respect" as a Goal

Respect is hard to quantify, and disrespect can be very subjective. For example, children are often told that they have had a "bad day." If asked, they will report (or be reported) as if they had been bad or disrespectful throughout the entire day. The report makes it sound as if nothing at all was positive in their behavior during the day. Had they screamed, argued, spit, bit, kicked, and hit from the first minute they arrived at school? Sometimes children behave fairly appropriately for most of the day but lose it later on, when they are

Although respect, positive behavior, community awareness, and social-emotional maturity are the greater goals of discipline, these are too complex for a behavior incentive plan.

tired. This becomes a "bad day." In other words, they received no credit whatsoever for the positive (or at least inoffensive) behavior during the rest of the day. One slipup lost them any credit, not only for their positive behavior but also for the energy and effort to be "good." Although respect, positive behavior, community awareness, and social-emotional maturity are the greater goals of discipline, these are too complex for a behavior incentive plan. However, remember that all of these things eventually come out of a successful behavior incentive plan.

Defining and Quantifying Desirable Behaviors

Adults need to be clear about the behaviors they want from children. Clear definitions of desirable behaviors include the following:

- "Put the toys and equipment back in their appropriate places."
- "Be sitting in the circle before I ring the bell."
- "Clear your desk before going to recess."
- "Hang your jacket on your own hook."

Certain behaviors can even be put into windows of time:

- "Be seated on the rug with your hands in your lap before the third ring of my bell."
- "Have all chores done by 9 o'clock."
- "Come to the circle when the big hand points to the three on the clock."

Quantify means "yes" or "no," not "sort of" or "later" or "intend to." "Kinda," "almost," or "sort of" do not work as quantifiable behaviors. A behavior is either done or not done. A behavior is either completed by a certain time or not.

Short-Term, Midterm, and Long-Term Goals

Through negotiation with the child, the adult sets short-term, midterm, and long-term goals. Short-term goals may be single, simple behavior changes. Midterm goals can be a set of behavior changes (all the behaviors for a good transition from one activity to another in the classroom routine). Long-term goals can be several sets of behaviors that promote overall positive school performance. The initial focus will be on short-term goals. However, midterm and long-term goals are essential to stretch children's sense of power and control over their lives. Developmentally, children may be focused on short-term issues and focus forward into only a relatively short period of time. However, the ability to focus on the future is a value of modern American culture. Being able to successfully anticipate skills needed for future benefit might be considered one definition of *wisdom*. As adults, we want children to keep the joy and spontaneity of childhood but also to recognize that what they do "now" affects what happens to them later.

Goals That Involve Time Frames

An initial goal for a second grader may involve, for example, successfully progressing through the tasks of a cleanup routine prior to going out to lunch. The set of tasks could consist of putting books back on shelves, returning supplies to a cabinet, putting completed or incomplete work into appropriate folders, picking up stray trash off of the floor, and being seated by a certain time. Unfortunately, if a behavior plan does not specify the amount of time each task should take, lunchtime may arrive with the child scrambling to finish the tasks in haphazard fashion. Set aside a time frame for each task. The following could be time frame guidelines for each task:

Quantify tasks and set up reasonable expectations so that there isn't a rush in the last 5 minutes to accomplish what requires 15 minutes or a half hour to do.

> Begin putting books and supplies away by 11:45 a.m. and finish by 11:50 a.m. If you finish by 11:50 a.m., then you have achieved the goal and will receive one point. If you are not finished by 11:50 a.m., then you will not receive one point.

Stick to the terms—and be merciless! If the child finishes organizing by 11:51, do not reward the point.

If children achieve some of the goals, they gain some of the points. If children achieve all of the goals, they gain all of the points, plus a bonus (to be discussed later). If this plan motivates children to improve the cleanup routine, they will also be developing habits that will be beneficial in the long-term. Once this goal is continually achieved, another goal—a more substantial goal—may be set. An extension of the cleanup routine to include other school activities and chores may be an appropriate new goal.

Remember, No Punishments

Punishments are not a part of this plan. Goals are accomplishments that must be met frequently and consistently. Once achieved, they result in rewards. Never take away any earned or achieved "points." In this plan, children never lose credit for achieved goals when they misbehave. This avoids the focus on punishment. The negative consequence of the lack of positive behaviors is that goals will be achieved slowly rather than quickly, and, as a result, *rewards will be slow to come.* The positive consequence of positive behavior is that goals will be achieved quickly and rewards gained quickly—and often. As the adult, you can be truly disappointed. You can freely express disappointment that children did not achieve their goals and did not earn their rewards. This expression can be honest and supportive, as opposed to punitive. There is no need to "tsk-tsk" the child or to rub it in.

> *Lack of positive behavior results in the lack of progress toward goals (and resultant rewards). However, the lack of, or relative infrequency of, positive behavior does not discredit the children's prior positive behavior.*

Children Should Choose Their Rewards (Within Reason)

Teachers pick goals based on insight about classroom tasks or routines that will benefit children in current and future situations. On the other hand, children are best at telling adults what motivates them in the "now." According to Marshall & Weisner (2004), students are constantly tuned into the radio station "WII-FM," or "What's In It For Me?" Avoid fighting or being angry at them for the lack of "appropriate" motivations but negotiate with them based on rewards they suggest. If children are motivated by toys, free time, certain privileges, or video games, then these should be the rewards. The principle is that these rewards have to be meaningful to the child—not to the adult. The child should be encouraged and led to minor, more substantial, and major rewards.

In the opening vignette, the dad decided that his son's rewards should be books because "books are good for him." Books would have been fine if they were something the boy enjoyed, but what the boy wanted was "Magic" cards. As a result, he lost interest in his dad's plan because his dad's rewards were not motivating to him. The dad might better have approached the situation by asking his son

"Would you be interested in a way to get a lot of cool stuff? And be in control of how fast you get it? Yes? Well, tell me what kind of things you'd like." For teachers trying these methods with children in the classroom, it's a good idea to coordinate rewards with parents or guardians.

Age-Appropriate and Individually Tailored Rewards

Rewards should be age-appropriate and tailored to the individual child. Adults have to put boundaries on the rewards, however, so that they are reasonably within the classroom or family budget. In a classroom, teachers have to deliver the instruction of their curriculum and meet the standards and expectations of the school. Special and/or extravagant rewards may not be realities for them. In addition, some children without behavior incentive plans may become jealous if they see a "bad" classmate being rewarded for behaviors they themselves consistently exhibit and are not rewarded for. These are sensitive issues. It's important to talk individually with children who express dissatisfaction and explain that everyone has different needs and requires different treatment. Make a conscious effort to appropriately praise all children for their good behavior, not only the ones who have experienced difficulty.

Rewarding Consistency With Bonuses

Great effort and sustained performance deserve greater rewards. If a child behaves better but does so only occasionally, you have not facilitated a major change. However, if the child behaves better over a longer period, he or she should receive a more substantial reward. You can build greater rewards into the incentive plan with the awarding of bonuses. *Bonus rewards* can consist of anything from more points, to money, to a special excursion or present. For example, the incentive plan can be set up so that each accomplishment—each completed behavior—results in one point credited (or stars on a chart). If all the behaviors in the set are completed, then bonus points are awarded. A certain number of points are gained when the set of behaviors is completed for one day. For a series of days and weeks of successful completion of behaviors, an even greater bonus should be rewarded.

Rewarding Frequency and Consistency

While each individual accomplishment deserves some credit, greater frequency deserves even greater credit. And consistency of positive behaviors deserves the highest reward. Some people feel that rewards in general make for artificial and inappropriate responses to good behavior. They assert that the real world doesn't reward people when they just do what they're supposed to do. But on the contrary, a well-designed behavior incentive plan does reflect the real world. For example, each time you go to work and do what you're required to do—a number of individual tasks—you get paid. If you go to work and do a good job frequently, you will get more pay and raises in pay. On top of that, if you go to work and do a good job consistently, then you will not only get raises but also get promotions.

> *A well-designed behavior incentive plan models habits and values that will promote success in the adult world.*

Examples of Rewards-Only Incentive Plans

The following are examples of rewards-only behavior incentive plans. There are different ways to design the plans. Four positive behaviors are shown in Example A, which is for younger children. Each *different positive behavior* gains a point. Example B, which is for older children, shows a single desirable positive behavior targeted (such as doing homework). Each *repetition of the positive behavior* is rewarded.

Example A

For a younger child, such as a kindergartner, the long-term goal should be about 1 week, but it could be just 1 day. For even younger or more impulsive children, the long-term goals may even be an hour or 2 of good behavior or the completion of a specific task a couple of times during the day. The following is an example of a set of goals:

Goals for School	Reward	Goals for Home
1. Hang up coat.	1 point	Use the toilet in the morning.
2. Put lunchbox away.	1 point	Brush teeth and wash face.
3. Place homework on teacher's desk.	1 point	Put on school clothes.
4. Be seated in the circle by the time the teacher rings the bell.	1 point	Put on socks and shoes.

With each of these goals completed, a point (or a star on a chart) is awarded. And a bonus would be given (three stars, for example) if all four of these morning transition tasks were accomplished within a reasonable time frame with a deadline. These can be paired with a dismissal transition set of goals or nighttime goals such as the following:

Goals for School	Reward	Goals for Home
1. Put toys and supplies away.	1 point	Take a bath.
2. Put homework in backpack.	1 point	Brush teeth and wash face.
3. Clear desk.	1 point	Change into pajamas.
4. Get coat and lunchbox.	1 point	Use the toilet and get into bed.

As with the morning set of goals, each completed goal earns a point (or a star on a chart). Also, a 3 point or star bonus can be awarded if all four tasks are accomplished within a reasonable time frame. With the accumulation of 10 points, the child may be allowed to have extra free time or an extra bedtime story if that is the reward that has been requested. If 14 points or stars are earned (which is the maximum possible: 4 points + 4 points + 3 points bonus + 3 points bonus), then a special sticker or computer or video time or whatever is desirable is awarded.

Example B

When the positive behavior has been repeated over a certain period of time (in this example, 1 week), a bonus is activated (five points). When the second, longer-term goal has been reached (2 weeks), a larger bonus is activated, and so on for additional goals (1 month and 6 months).

If the targeted behavior goals are achieved every day for one month,

- A single point is gained for each of the 30 days (30 points).
- Four 5-point bonuses are awarded for each of four 1-week goals achieved (4×5 = plus 20 points).
- Two 10-point bonuses are gained for each of two 2-week goals achieved (2×10 = plus 20 points).
- One 20-point bonus is gained for one 1-month goal achieved (1×20 = plus 20 points).

Thus 30 + 20 + 20 + 20 = 90 points gained.

Occurrence is rewarded each time, but frequency and consistency are more richly rewarded. This is a more complex behavior incentive plan more suitable for children who can understand the mathematics involved, such as second graders or older.

Rewards-Only Behavior Plan

Points	Reward
5 points	Extra 15 minutes computer time or free play, or pick from prize jar
10 points	30 minutes control of computer game, or comic book, or new markers
50 points	Line leader for the day, makes choice for snack, or pizza day
100 points	CD or video game gift, lunch from fast-food restaurant, or magazine subscription
500 points	Special field trip for class of child's choice, or boom box

How Points Are Earned

	1 Day	1 week bonus	2 week bonus	1 month bonus	6 months
	1 point	5 points	10 points	20 points	100 points
6 days desired behavior	6 points				
1 week desired behavior total = 12 points	7 points	5 points			
2 weeks desired behavior total = 34 points	14 points	5+5 points			
3 weeks desired behavior total = 46 points	21 points	5+5+5 points	10 points		
1 month desired behavior	30	5+5+5+5	10+10	20	90 points
2 months desired behavior	60 185 points	5+5+5+5+ 5+5+5+5+5	10+10+ 10+10	20+20	
6 months desired behavior	183 663 points	5+5+5+5+5+5 5+5+5+5+5 5+5+5+5+5 5+5+5+5+5 5+5+5+5+5	10+10+10+10+ 10+10+10+10+ 10+10+10+10+ 10	20+20+20+ 20+20+20	100

The 6 months of desired behavior earns 663 total points. The 663 points are made up of

183 points for each of the 183 days,

plus twenty-six 5-point bonuses for each of the twenty-six weeks,

plus thirteen 10-point bonuses for each of the thirteen 2-week periods,

plus six 20-point bonuses for each of the six 1-month periods,

plus the final 100-point bonus for the 6-month period.

During the same 6 months, someone might not have performed desired behavior for the entire period. Thus they will not earn some of the bonuses and will have a lower overall point total.

Note: Totals are cumulative. That is, the total is accurate under the premise that no points are traded for rewards prior to the achievement of the goals.

- Frequency and/or consistency should be rewarded.
- The greater the goal, the greater the reward. Achieving minor goals should result in minor rewards; more substantial goals have more substantial rewards; major goals have major rewards.
- Children choose rewards (through negotiation with adults).
- Adults choose goals (through negotiation with children).

As mentioned in the previous chapter, don't expect a plan to change children overnight. It will take time to achieve success, so don't give up on the plan or the children. Chances are that they will do things differently—and still be difficult. It will be up to you to make adaptations as needed. In other words, you, the adult, are still the major ingredient in this plan: your awareness, sensitivity, creativity, wisdom, and flexibility. You still need to be the teacher or parent! This means that you must observe carefully and then respond to children's sometimes unpredictable behavior.

The underlying principles of a behavior incentive plan are sound and appropriate. The plan will give children appropriate feedback depending on what they do. Failure to follow through will not be rewarded. Minor achievements will be rewarded with minor gifts. Exceptional compliance or achievement will be rewarded exceptionally. With the contract established, the job of the adult is simply to follow through and pay attention.

Always Follow Through

Another way to sabotage the contract, besides getting angry, is to save the child from enduring the consequences of misbehaving. Do not save children from getting or not getting their due consequences. Oppositional children can be very manipulative. They tend to be experts at getting adults to change the contract, to "save" them from the choices they have made. Don't let them manipulate you. To "save" children from the results of their choices, you effectively undermine them and any possibility that they will develop a sense of responsibility. Sometimes when we very much want a child to do well, we make certain concessions, but this is not in the child's true best interest. *Remember, a behavior incentive plan is part of a larger process of discipline.* It normally will not work in and of itself if there are other major issues. Sometimes, however, it is just the tool to shift the balance of negativity that has plagued your classroom since the first day of school.

Remember the Underlying Principles

To design and use a behavior incentive plan, it is critical that you understand the underlying principles. Most behavior incentive plans, whether casual or formal, fail because people do not understand the true goals of the plans. Subsequently, they fail to design the plans correctly.

You must have appropriate expectations, set clear goals, and reward children fairly, then implement the plan and watch the change that occurs over the course of several weeks and months. When you know the change you want to bring about and how to go about it, you can anticipate how children are going to act, and so what they do is not as surprising or disruptive to you. In this state, teachers develop what Rick Smith (2004) has called an "inner authority": in essence, a confidence that cannot be shaken by children who resist disciplinary action. You can then feel certain that you're moving from being a good teacher to a great teacher. Isn't that what you want to be? And don't children deserve our greatness? That is how children become great teens, great adults, and great citizens.

Chapter Highlights

- Goals and rewards are interrelated; however, adults desire behavior goals from children, while children desire rewards from adults.
- Adults should set goals with children's input. The underlying principles of goals need to reflect the expectations and standards of society.

- Behaviors and goals need to be concrete and quantifiable. There should be no judgment calls as to whether a goal has been achieved; it must be obvious.
- Short-term, midterm, and long-term goals need to be set.
- Children should pick rewards that are meaningful to them (with adult guidance or negotiation). Rewards also need to be age-appropriate.
- Each occurrence of targeted behavior deserves some reward. Greater frequency deserves greater rewards. Consistency deserves the greatest reward.
- Stay with the plan. Don't "save" children from their choices by giving unearned rewards.
- Do not expect great initial results. There is often tremendous negative momentum to overcome. This is a tool in a larger process of discipline. It is not a magic wand.
- Instinct and intuition can lead to good choices, but conceptual clarity allows for proactive choices and moves people to make great choices.

PART V

Recognizing and Responding to Specific Behaviors and Emotions

"Sorry I can't stay --- I'm late for emoting, and then I have anger management."

ider issues
t Sylwester
to a body—
tudents are
ɛm" (p. 10).
d's life. Just
family as a
ctors at the
f the issues
iate profes-
But before
the subjec-
ɔarents) can
s problems.
ᴀake formal
issues that
to develop
d may need

4

**here Is
to It**

h Deeper Issues

loss?

ist?

teachers can
ɛntions with
chapter will
ɛnxious, fear-
se these feel-
ɛcognize the
r additional

act out from
indicative of

ɛ doesn't do it all the time, but it's
's something that he's done for a
: this too, but not as often . . . not
ɹight . . . that he'll grow out of? I
: teacher from last year mentioned
: his preschool teacher mentioned
tor teacher said something about
same, and then had some kind of
that bad. Do you think it is okay
ɹould be worried about? Is there
t I should bring up to his parents?

ɔncerned that a more serious
ɛhaviors. Sometimes it's clear
ɛs it isn't. If there is a problem,
can handle it, whether it will
use danger to the child or other

children in the classroom. Teachers may need to con
beyond what is observable in the classroom. As Robe
(2003) wrote, "Misbehavior is to a classroom what pain is
Much classroom behavior is . . . diagnostic. Acting-out
informing the teacher that the lesson isn't working with th

Misbehavior may reflect some deeper issue in the chi
as therapists may need to consider the dynamics of the
whole, the teacher may need to address all potential f
systemic level inside and outside of the classroom. Or
are beyond the scope of the classroom teacher, an approp
sional referral for specialized assistance must be made
jumping ahead to dangerously provocative assumption
tive intuition, wisdom, and experience of teachers (and
be activated to guide the process of identifying seriou
Although teachers cannot and should not attempt to
diagnoses, if they have a deeper understanding of the
exhibit as bad behavior, they will be better equipped
appropriate classroom interventions or decide that a chi
a referral for professional assessment and diagnosis.

This chapter addresses a set of questions:

1. Is this an angry child?

2. Is this a sad child?

3. Is this a fearful or anxious child?

4. Is this a child who is holding unprocessed pain or

5. Is this a child who may need a referral to a specia

With the first four questions, there are interventions
try in the classroom first. Or they may try such interv
professional assessment and assistance if necessary. Thi
look at how to recognize if a child is indeed angry, sad,
ful, or in pain and explore what teachers can do to decre
ings and emotions. The fifth question helps teachers
behaviors that should alert them to refer children f
services.

Happy Children Act Out Too

It's important to keep in mind that even happy children
time to time and that their behavior is not necessarily

deeper problems. A happy child can be a goofy child. A happy child can be an active child. A happy child may at times lose control, have a temper tantrum, get into fights, and become sad, anxious, fearful, and angry. A happy child may exhibit occasional odd behavior or even periods of odd behavior and misbehavior. However, a happy child is usually able to receive and respond to everyday discipline and support; that is, their negativity or bad behavior does not persist. Classroom management, adult support, and guidance will be sufficient to handle the behavioral, educational, emotional, and social challenges of these kids.

Be sensitive to the needs of happy children, monitor their actions and how they change, but don't make too much of what are probably typical childhood behaviors. By paying attention to them, you'll see that their misbehavior likely stems from specific situations, changes in physical conditions, disruptions in routines, temperamental traits, or the dynamics of social situations. Negative responses to these situations do not represent deep-seated issues. Recognizing this, you can keep your energy focused on the children who do need more attention and need you to look to the real reasons underlying their behavior.

Is This an Angry Child?

Anger may manifest itself in the form of temper tantrums, hypersensitivity (excessive or abnormal sensitivity), and hypervigilance (excessive alertness or watchfulness). Or it may be recognized in moodiness or sullenness toward everyone and everything. When it does come out, anger may be expressed as an indiscriminate ferocity that is disproportionate to the situation or transgression against the child. This is not the same as

> *It is important to remember that anger is a normal, healthy, and positive energy, if properly expressed.*

children who can and do get angry at times. Everyone gets angry at times. Everyone experiences situations in which getting angry is the most natural response. Anger empowers individuals to take the risks that they would otherwise be too fearful to consider. Anger gives people the energy to challenge the things that need to be challenged in order to have a healthy and secure life. Telling children "Don't be so angry! I don't see why you're so angry!" disables them from the energy that allows them to take care of themselves—and gives them the courage to fight for self-preservation. It is more appropriate to acknowledge that the anger comes from a place that seeks to be respected. Anger in response to mistreatment or provocation is natural. However, if you have a child who is consistently angry, with or without provocation, then you are wise to have a greater level of concern and to think that you may have an "angry" child in your classroom.

To Respond or Not to Respond

Many educators advise against giving children attention when their anger escalates, as it may serve little more than to distract both the teacher and the class from the intended purpose at the time. Lee Canter (1992) warned teachers to "ignore the covert hostility of a student" (p. 180), to defuse the situation and bring about student compliance. But ignoring a child's anger may cause the child to feel that his or her essential self and worth are being ignored. This can intensify the anger and thus intensify the negative behavior—just the opposite of what is desired!

Anger may be a key issue in understanding and improving mental health and, as a result, behavior. Some children carry anger consistently in their bodies, facial expressions, attitudes, values, beliefs, and behaviors. Or the anger lies just beneath the surface, building over days, weeks, months, or even years. A small transgression or a great offense can equally set off the anger from within. Many people, including children, may not even realize on a conscious level that they are still angry; they may think they've "let it go." In such cases, "letting it go" actually means they have taken the issue, squeezed it, and crushed it into a hard nugget of bitterness that they dropped onto a pile of resentment growing inside.

Many people may not even be aware of the anger growing inside of them, thinking they've "let it go."

Anger Alerts Us to Something Deeper

When a child begins to get angry, how do you react? What do you say? "Calm down." "Don't be so emotional." "Don't get so mad." "Get a hold of yourself." "Let's not get too excited." "Let's not get carried away." While everyone says these things sometimes, the command assumes that children (and adults too) have choice and control over emotions such as anger. They also assume that the emotions are inherently negative, rather than purposeful. Both assumptions are incorrect and dangerous. As Robert Sylwester (2003) explained,

> *Emotion* is a general term for a complex, critically important . . . arousal system that unconsciously interprets and evaluates

sensory information, thus alerting us to current and potential dangers and opportunities that reach our emotional threshold, . . . Furthermore, we don't consciously choose to become emotionally aroused, and such arousal often interferes with what we're currently doing. In effect, our emotions tell us to stop doing what we're doing and to attend to this more important challenge. . . . A sudden emotional stimulus can thus easily and immediately stop classroom activity—and it's then neurologically difficult to get folks to rationally shut off their emotional arousal and resume what they are doing. It's best to realize that the disruptive emotional arousal will continue until the problem is resolved and to simply take the time to resolve it before resuming the previous activity. (pp. 38–39)

Emotions are not only personal warnings of issues that need to be addressed for the individual, but, to an astute adult, they can also be an alert to a child's need. Ignoring or attempting to suppress the emotion is difficult and also dismissive. Sylwester was both compassionate and practical when he recommended taking the time in the classroom to resolve the problem before resuming the previous activity. The danger is that the child may not have understood the instructions and is confused or is concerned that he or she will be left behind or left out. Responding to the cue will often prevent the problem from developing.

For some individuals, however, the "problem" that led to the angry response is far more pervasive in depth and breadth than just the behavior that manifests in the classroom. With angry children, the confusion or the fear of being left behind or left out may be symbolic of more profound and painful prior experiences. If the adult notices an emotional reaction that is disproportionate to the specific and current situation, then the adult should consider that prior distress or trauma could be playing a role in the behavior.

Anger Is the Secondary Emotion

It is important to remember that anger is normally not the primary emotion, but the secondary emotion. Before there is anger, there is an underlying emotion—an emotion that asks for an act of self-preservation, increased security, and nurturing. Anger tends to be expressed more often in boys and men because they tend to go through a cultural

> *The powerful secondary emotion of anger is usually preceded by a primary vulnerable emotion.*

socialization process that disconnects them from their vulnerable feelings. This is apparent in the plot of virtually every action movie in recent decades. Think about it: Shortly after the beginning of the movie, someone very close to the hero (mother, girlfriend, sibling) has been horribly killed. As he holds his dying (fill in the blank), he suffers tremendous anguish, with tears streaming down his face. After the dear one dies, the finality of the death hits him, and his despair intensifies—for about 30 seconds! Then he raises his head up, with tears still fresh on his face; his jaw sets, and his eyes turn hard. The rest of the movie spirals from his cold, hard anger and the determination to avenge the wrongful death. Such a plot clearly demonstrates anger as a secondary emotion—and a byproduct of the male training that vulnerable feelings are to be suppressed rather than expressed, except perhaps in anger and violence.

Teachers Can Offer a Reparative Opportunity

If you have an angry child in your class, you can begin to address the issue by identifying the emotion or issue underneath the anger, stopping the negative behavior, and then teaching the child how to express anger in appropriate and healthy ways. However, some children's issues are so deep and complex that they are beyond the scope, knowledge, and responsibility of most teachers. Children who are victims of abuse, molestation, or other maltreatment may need many levels of intervention to succeed in the classroom and beyond. Teachers should not try to be therapists, and they should not consider themselves failures if they can't turn every angry child into a happy child. However, teachers are in a unique position to develop reparative relationships with children.

A reparative relationship is a relationship that allows the person who has been betrayed or wounded to risk and trust, to care and to be cared for, and to hope.

In the classroom, teachers expect that they will teach and in some cases develop close relationships with certain children. Reparative relationships are critical for certain children who need their teachers to go beyond the role of instructor and to "be there" to listen to emotional and psychological concerns. Teachers who seek to understand the origins of negative behavior, and try to understand and love the child rather than simply reject him or her, become available for reparative relationships. As Harry Wong (1991) noted, "You may be the only stable adult your students will ever see in their lifetime. You may be their only hope and dream for a brighter tomorrow."

The Appropriate Expression of Anger

These are some ways children can be helped to express anger appropriately:

- Verbalization
- Writing
- Problem solving
- Negotiation

It also may be appropriate to work from an incremental orientation. Although teachers do not ordinarily want children yelling at each other, a child who yells instead of hits has made a significant positive incremental change in the behavior improvement process. After all, foot stomping on the floor is much better than stomping on another child. When children have successfully moved from hitting to yelling, the teacher can direct further incremental change, such as verbalizing with intensity but without yelling and threats: "I really don't like what you did. Don't do it again." When that method of communication has been established, the next step would be verbalization with lower intensity, more overt problem-solving attempts, and so on.

Of course, many teachers and parents want to move a child directly to the most civilized process. However, for angry children, the downward spiral into anger was itself a gradual and incremental process. They went from mild complaints, to loud complaints, to loud complaints accompanied by rants and raves, to severe acting out. Undoing this pattern does not happen magically or without sustained effort.

Is This a Sad Child?

Anger is secondary to various primary vulnerable feelings. These vulnerabilities are not always covered up by anger. Sadness, another easily observable emotion, communicates the heaviness a child carries within. Normally, when people think about someone being sad or depressed, they consider two very different manifestations: the "blues" and clinical depression. The blues involve "normal" sadness or disappointment that occurs occasionally throughout the course of life. A person

The blues, in the form of fleeting sadness or depression, pass as other feelings and experiences (which are relatively rewarding and meaningful) reassert themselves.

may be disappointed, disempowered, dismissed, disrespected, devalued, insulted or impugned, or frustrated by others' actions or by his or her own behavior. The resultant sadness or depression is transitory. *Major depression* involves a clinical diagnosis. Children and adults who have major depression are virtually unable to function. The depression is so pervasive that they are often unable to make the simplest decisions or even get out of bed in the morning. Profound feelings of low self-esteem, self-hatred, helplessness, and hopelessness dominate. Often a deep sense of humiliation for having such negative feelings can move such afflicted individuals toward suicidal thinking or suicide. Children with clinical depression require the guidance and monitoring of a mental health professional.

Living Life in a Fog

Children who experience fleeting sadness or clinical depression are fairly easy to recognize, though they are on opposite ends of the spectrum. But what about the child in class who seems to be living life in a fog, walking around as if carrying a weight but still managing to complete tasks? Will he or she "snap out of it"? Is there a specific cause? The clinical term for this type of depression is dysthymic disorder. People with this disorder are largely functional at home and in school or work. However, their achievements ring hollow, as there is no stable sense of growth or underlying pride. The clinical definition for children assumes at least 1 year of "walking dead" or "living life in a fog." There is usually some significant and enduring dysfunction in the family or other major system (which could be the school). Trauma or excessive stress may be the source of the ongoing dread or sadness. A child may have a parent who is mentally ill, alcoholic, emotionally disconnected, or abusive. In school, a child could experience being bullied, academic failure, unfulfilling relationships, secret pain, and so forth. Such children may or may not act out.

Childhood Expression of Dysthymic Depression

It is often difficult to recognize this kind of depression in children, as they express it in a variety of ways, both classic and not. For young ones, just about any change in behavior can be an indication of depression. However, there are usually several areas of change in a child's behavior, rather than a single change. Isolated changes are often a normal part of childhood development. Of course, if the change is particularly disturbing (traumatic), a single change might be indicative of a problem that should be investigated and attended to.

Some children have such enduring (low-level, without severe acting out) negative experiences from so early in their lives that they do not know anything else. They can step into a classroom with little or no expectation that anything will be any better. They don't expect to like school or to like the teacher or their classmates. They either go through the motions or test all the boundaries by acting without self-restraint. They may or may not create chaos and disruption in the classroom and the playground. They don't care about what others feel and experience because they feel that no one cares about them. Yet such children may make reasonable progress in school. Some will never draw attention to themselves; some will explode later in life as adolescents or adults with pent-up frustration.

Not Sure If They Matter

Cameron was a very attractive child who drew other children and adults to him. He was extremely bright, very charming, and also quite articulate. He was funny and fun to be with. Suddenly, and without apparent provocation, he would hit children or become explosively defiant with the teacher. Cameron's teacher could not see that he was a sad child. Later, she learned that Cameron's mother was permanently disabled for psychological reasons. She was the mother of three other children from three different fathers. She could not take care of Cameron, and so he had been placed in a foster home. He had tentatively bonded with his foster parents (two very caring and loving people) but was conflicted as he received inconsistent messages from his mother that she wanted him but could not get him back. Accepted, rejected, abandoned, included, excluded, loved, ignored, indulged, neglected, and never knowing what it would be next, Cameron was never really sure if he mattered. His underlying sadness and insecurity about his value caused him to need to test other adults to see if they really cared for him. Every once in awhile, the sadness would surge forward as anger, and he would act out severely.

Problem Solving With Sadness

When you suspect a child in your class might be sad or depressed, the first thing you can do is show interest in the child and talk about the sadness. The mere fact of being interested in why the child is sad is validating to the child. Extreme sadness often makes children believe that there is something wrong with them. Because they cannot make themselves happy, they believe that sadness is somehow their choice. Sometimes the most powerful intervention and feedback is the acknowledgment that difficulties can make people feel deep sadness and that it would be unusual not to be deeply sad or depressed under the circumstances.

Acknowledge and support the child and his or her life and experiences, saying, "That must make you really sad." While examining the deeper issues and beginning to address them, always validate the child. Problem solving the underlying issues for sadness can sometimes make all the difference in the world. Some of these issues can be significantly addressed by teachers, while others may require other interventions.

> *Acknowledgment and acceptance of the sadness may be confirmation and attention that the child has not previously received.*

Is This a Fearful or Anxious Child?

When child has a fear, he or she fears a specific thing, situation, experience, or person. In some ways, fear is easy to handle. If a child is afraid of snakes, there are two relatively simple approaches to dealing with the fear:

1. Avoid snakes: no snakes, no fear—no fear, no problem.

2. Facilitate systematic desensitization to snakes: This means bringing children gradually into ever-increasing proximity to snakes, with the children maintaining control over exactly how much exposure they experience. This can be done casually and instinctively, or more overtly and purposefully. In time, fear can be overcome or made manageable.

Of course, the natural tendency for most people, including children, is to *avoid* their fears. However, in avoiding fear, it often becomes more and more intense and more and more overwhelming and intimidating. When this happens, fear can dominate a person's life. If you have a fearful child in your class, you need to determine whether the fear is imagined, a product of inexperience, or is reality or experience based.

Imaginary Fear or Fear From Unfamiliarity

If the fear is imaginary or a consequence of inexperience, then a process of systematic desensitization is advised. A child entering kindergarten who has never been in a classroom situation may be terrified of the newness and strangeness. By coming to school every day, there will be a systematic desensitization as each day is survived. Teacher support, fun activities, and play with other children should help to extinguish the fear as the unfamiliarity of kindergarten diminishes. If a child fears coming to school, it is critical to communicate to parents that they must continue to bring the child to school and that the child cannot get used to school without being at school. A "break" or a couple days off from school will not help the child. In this situation, the fear has no basis in reality, and so regular doses of reality (daily attendance) become the logical and effective antidote to the fear.

Real, Experience-Based Fear

If the fear has a basis in reality, such as bullying on the playground, then the child needs the teacher's help or perhaps the help of other professionals to appropriately address the threat. Teachers can help children begin to overcome fear with both advice and action. If a child is indeed being bullied, the teacher should not only talk to the child being bullied and offer comfort, but must discipline the children doing the bullying. In some situations, a more aggressive, coordinated, programwide intervention program may be required.

Can and should children overcome particular fears? It depends on both their developmental stage and the nature of the fear. Should fearful children be expected to use the restroom by themselves? Or to try something new? Support children's efforts to confront their fears but respect that they may need a significant amount of time and support to be successful.

Anxiety Is Nonspecific Fear

An anxious child is different from a fearful child. Unlike a fearful person, an anxious person does not have a specific source or object for their anxiety. Anxiety is amorphous and undifferentiated. Anxiety is fear without direction, and thus without remedy. Everyone has experiences of anxiety that cause distress. However, normal anxiety tends to be more momentary or confined to a time period. One ponders and tries to anticipate possible and probable, foreseeable and unforeseeable, challenges or difficulties in a coming task or experience. Children may be anxious that others won't like them or that they won't like school. If asked why others won't like them or what part of school it is that worries them, they don't know: "Something bad—I don't know what—might happen!"

Too Much Anxiety

Eric Jensen (1997) argued that low stress is one of the criteria of optimal learning. Donna Walker Tileston (2004) defined stress or threats according to the following categories:

- *Physical threats,* which come from inside or outside the classroom
- *Emotional threats,* such as the fear of being embarrassed
- *Education threats,* such as fear of failure or of not understanding the material well enough to carry out tasks
- *Limited resources,* ranging from a lack of language or verbal skills to unrealistic deadlines for work, which restrict the student's ability to be successful

Stress is supposed to alert humans to potential threats or dangers. Anxiety is connected to the survival instinct, helping people to be aware, sensitive, and vigilant, just in case there may be some danger ahead. The question "Is this an anxious child?" does not refer to this normal and occasional anxiety. An anxious child is one with *too much anxiety.* Children want to survive. They want to have fun and want to do things and have things and, as such, may naturally have some anxiety. Some children, however, come to the classroom already in constant state of anxiety and then stay in that constant state of anxiety. Anxious children are not sensitive and vigilant, but rather hypersensitive and hypervigilant, in response to a great sense of vulnerability and a lack of ability to protect themselves. When the body stays in a constant state of anxiety or stress—stays in the fight-or-flight mode—physiological demands can wear the body down. A multitude of physical problems and a propensity for emotional and psychological problems may develop.

Safety, Stability, and Predictability in the Classroom

Sometimes the relative stability and predictability of the teacher, the classroom, and the classroom routines allow an otherwise anxious child to feel secure. Many children love school because it is so much more calm, predictable, and safe than a chaotic or dysfunctional home. It may even surprise you to learn that life is chaotic at home, because these children can be so orderly and organized in your classroom.

How does a creative, flexible, and spontaneous teacher affect anxious children? How
does deviating from the classroom routine and
schedule to capitalize on "teachable moments"
affect anxious children? Such changes in the
classroom routine may be highly disruptive to
such children. You certainly can and should
seize wonderful moments to be creative and
flexible. However, be aware of and support the
more anxious children. Give them more reas-

Is your classroom an anxious classroom? Are your routines and reactions predictable? The calm and peace of your classroom will allow children to be "ready to learn" instead of "ready to cringe."

surance, especially during changes in routine. If you notice that your
extra attention and consideration does not visibly decrease anxiety,
consider seeking guidance and support from the administration,
family members, or a mental health professional.

Family Influence on Anxiety

Parents and guardians can be overvigilant
and overprotective, which often creates hypersensitivity and hypervigilance in children.
Have you noticed that many of the more
anxious, hypersensitive, and hypervigilant
children have very anxious, hypersensitive,
and hypervigilant parents? Such parents give
constant covert messages to their children
that they are in danger and that they are vul-

Anxiety is modeled and taught. Anxious children need to be supported and protected but also encouraged to develop their strengths, skills, and resources.

nerable to unexpected harm. A child who is chronically anxious tends
to come from one or both of the following life experiences:

- Chronic caregiver anxiety that transmits messages of one's
  innate vulnerability
- Unpredictability and lack of power and control that result in
  frequent negative consequences

Talking With Families

Teachers need to talk to parents and guardians of anxious
children to discover whether their hypersensitivity and hypervigilance have made their children anxious. Do children feel safe at
home? Is there instability, distress, unpredictable and arbitrary discipline, or other threatening and intimidating dynamics in the family?
If so, there is not only a need to help and support the child but
also a need to work with family members. Teachers need to inform

parents that the conditions they are creating at home may prevent the child from being ready to learn in school. Stability, predictability, routine, schedules, and other indicators and characteristics of attentive nurturing decrease anxiety. Teachers need to encourage parents to bring their children to school on time every day, to read regularly together, and so forth. These functional recommendations serve to alleviate anxiety. Sometimes teachers need to teach parents how to support the child, while being careful not to tell parents how to parent.

Is This a Child Who Is Holding Unprocessed Pain or Loss?

Adults tend to think of childhood as an idyllic time, when life is sweet and wonderful. They sometimes believe that children are oblivious to the harshness and cruelties of the world. Adults often try to shield children from the painful, ugly things in the world. However, children, in their own developmentally defined ways, may experience devastating losses and great pain in the course of ordinary life. Sometimes the losses are recognized by adults, such as the passing away of a beloved grandmother or grandfather; moving from a house, neighborhood, school, or community; or the loss of a friend who moves away. Sometimes the losses are unexpected, such as a young life lost in a car accident, a financial crisis, or a diagnosis of a medical disability. People suffer pain with losses, but some people suffer alone in silence. Children model themselves after the adults in their lives. Subsequently, some children suffer alone in silence as well.

Stuck in Pain

Children, like adults, go through the grieving process: denial, anger, bargaining, depression, and acceptance (Kübler-Ross, 1969). However, when they do not, have not, or are not allowed to go through the process of grief and loss, they often find themselves stuck in pain. If children are told to "be tough" or "just get through it," they may not deal with their pain, unaware of any other way to process it. These children need to be supported in expressing their losses and pain and to be given permission to acknowledge that there has been a loss, even if their parents (as models) do not acknowledge the loss.

Supporting Children as They Work Through Pain

Davie and Emily are two children who experienced the death of a parent. Davie, a 2-year-old at the time, was barely verbal. His mother died in a car accident. The surviving family included him, his father, an older brother, and an older sister. At his day care, he found a family set of stuffed toy dogs. His teacher sat with him every time he played with the dogs. Each day, he took out the stuffed toy dogs from their tub. He placed them carefully on the table, one by one, speaking in his high, little voice. He said, "This is the daddy dog," as he placed the biggest toy dog on the table. Then he said, "This is the mommy dog," as he placed the next-largest dog on the table. "This is the big brother dog. . . ." and so on through the rest of the dog family. Every day for weeks, Davie played with the dogs. And every time, he laid the mommy dog down on its side and said, "Mommy dog died." It broke the teacher's heart to watch the boy process his mother's death in this way, but she recognized the importance of supporting and allowing him to experience grief.

Emily was 5 years old when her father died from cancer. In her preschool class, she used crayons to draw the same picture, over and over, for 4 months. She drew her father lying down at the bottom of the paper. Then she drew fluffy white clouds and a bright yellow sun at the top of the paper. She drew a green tree on the right side of the paper. Finally, she drew the brown ground on the bottom edge of the paper, covering up her drawing of her father, and announced, "Daddy got buried." Her teacher found it difficult to be with Emily while she did this, but stayed and watched her continue drawing. She knew Emily needed to draw the picture. One day, Emily drew the picture differently. She started with the white fluffy clouds and a bright yellow sun in the sky. Then she drew the green tree. Then she drew the brown ground. Then she drew her father up in the sky above the clouds and announced, "Daddy is in heaven now." The little girl, by drawing her picture over and over, had finally found a place in her heart and soul to hold the memory of her father.

Don't Let Discomfort Lead to Interference

It would not have been surprising if teacher discomfort had caused interference with the children's grieving processes. Although losses may stay with children throughout life, they are more likely to be able to carry them in a safe and positive place in their hearts and souls if they have been allowed to grieve in their own way. If you see or feel deep pain or darkness in a child, give feedback to parents so that permission and support may be gained to process that pain or loss at home, too.

The parents may not be giving themselves or their child that permission. Or they may not be aware of the depth of their child's suffering. Whether and how parents support their children through the grieving process is their decision. However, professional and responsible teachers must communicate and offer observations, expertise, education, and experience to support the welfare of children in their classrooms. Sharing feedback is not an educator's decision: It is an educator's duty.

Is This a Child Who May Need a Referral to a Specialist?

This is the most sensitive and the most threatening question. This is the question that teachers are afraid to ask—and to answer. Parents are terrified that teachers and administrators may answer in the affirmative. Most people are not educated, trained, or experienced enough to diagnose specific cognitive, physical, neurological, educational, emotional, vocational, and other specialized challenges. However, everyone has ample experience with the range of "normal" behavior. From this instinct of what constitutes normal behavior comes an intuitive recognition of *behavior that is outside the range of normal experience.* Usually, people will not be able to name what the issue might be or even to identify specifically what is unusual or different. However, they can note that something is "off" about someone's behavior. It might be the way someone

- holds his or her body,
- moves when he or she walks,
- has a "look" in the eyes,
- makes odd associations with words or thoughts,
- has a consistent inconsistency,
- experiences difficulty with a task or idea that shouldn't be difficult,
- is unable to retain or learn information,
- has unexpected strength in some areas and unexpected weakness in others,
- has a developmental inconsistency,
- has odd reactions, and so forth.

"Off" Is Not Wrong

When something "off" is noticed and is repeated over time, it does not mean that something is wrong with a child. It means that the issue needs to be assessed by someone with greater experience and expertise. Professionals with specific training are better equipped to recognize and pinpoint a child's issue and suggest appropriate interventions. Knowledge is empowering, and a clinical diagnosis (if necessary) can help both the child and family receive needed services—and may save a child years of frustration and failure. As mentioned earlier, you have not failed if you cannot identify a child's specific problem. Sometimes only a specialist can do this.

Undiagnosed learning disabilities, neurological issues, auditory or visual deficits, vocational challenges, developmental delays, physical challenges, cognitive processes, family stress, and any other undiagnosed issue can doom a child to a lifetime of unnecessary suffering. It is daunting and even terrifying for parents to consider that their child might have special needs. All parents want their children to be at least normal, if not exceptional. The possibility that their child may have some special challenge may cause parents to experience the grieving process themselves, beginning (and lasting for quite some time) with denial. Most teachers have had the experience of telling a parent that something needs to be investigated further. There is something about the child's functioning that is unusual or different or unexpected. Perhaps there is some mismatch between ability and performance. Parents may respond with tremendous resistance, if not outright anger.

> *Parents want teachers to tell them about their children. But oftentimes they are terrified they will be told something they don't want to hear.*

Communicating Concern to Parents

A preschool director observed that Shelley, a 4-year-old girl, did not respond to other children or teachers with the same alertness as the other 4-year-old children. There was a flatness in the tone of her voice when she described what she was doing or what she wanted to do. She had difficulty maintaining eye contact. She would get extremely distressed when minor things didn't go her way. She would cry and scream as if she'd been stuck with a knife. She still had frequent toileting accidents. The director was not sure why Shelley behaved this way, although he was sure something was unusual. He spoke to her parents about it and was basically ignored. He continued to observe Shelley and decided to speak with the parents again. This time, the director used a three-point strategy that proved to be useful and effective:

- Data/observations
- Interpretations
- Recommended interventions

Do not begin a conversation with parents with your own interpretations or recommendations for interventions, such as "I believe that your son has an auditory-processing learning disability" or "I think your son needs to see a speech and language specialist." Such recommendations and interpretations are filled with negative implications. Parents may react with fear and pain as a result, followed immediately by denial and defensiveness. Defensiveness is often expressed in attacking comments, such as "Are you a therapist? You're not qualified to make that diagnosis. You never liked my child."

Start With Data or Observations

Before talking with parents, compile a list of data or observations about their child over a significant length of time. Begin the conversation with the statement "These are some things that I have noticed about your child." Since these are your observations of and experiences with the child, there is no real avenue for denial on the part of the parent. This is the raw data from your time observing and interacting with the child. The preschool director mentioned earlier had a written list of 20 observations for Shelley's parents, including the following:

- Shelley has toilet accidents at least once a day.
- Shelley looks away when you are talking to her directly—she has trouble keeping eye contact, even if you ask her to look you directly in the eye.
- When you come up from behind her and call her name, she virtually jumps out of her skin in an exaggerated, startled response.
- When upset, she will suck her thumb and rock herself.
- When asked what she had for dinner, she talked about the dog.
- She often watches the children play but does not participate herself.
- She spills her milk or juice very often.
- She eats with her fingers, even when utensils are available and appropriate.

When you present a series of observations or other data, they tend to be less vulnerable to parental challenge and you're less likely to be interrupted. You saw what you saw, and you heard what you heard. If, however, you try to present a series of interpretations (even if you are absolutely certain they are correct), they are open to challenge. For example, an interpretation such as "Shelley seems a bit immature" may invite arguments about the following:

- The relative maturity of Shelley versus other children
- The individual developmental process of maturity
- Unrealistic versus realistic teacher expectations of children
- The sensitivity versus the insensitivity of teachers regarding Shelley
- The amount of effort that parents have put into Shelley
- How much the parents really care
- Whether parents or teachers are the real experts about Shelley

Take care not to make a major strategic error with your presentation. Always present data and observations first, both in oral and written form. Having these things written down is particularly powerful. It is not meant to be a formal document, but rather a list on a piece of paper without any title or identifying information. In Shelley's case, her parents responded first with hostile expressions, but gradually their expressions changed to those of sadness and great concern. When the director finished with the list, he asked them, "There have been other things, too. But I made up this list to give you an idea of what we have been observing in Shelley. Do any of these things sound familiar to you? Have you observed or experienced these things with Shelley at home?"

Only at School?

In this particular case, the parents were able to acknowledge that they had experienced the same things at home with Shelley. Sometimes parents will deny that anything like what you've noticed has happened at home or in previous classrooms or schools. Their implication is that the behavior occurs in only your classroom and is connected to the (poor) way in which you teach and discipline. The accusation is that it is all your fault, if not merely a figment of your imagination or insensitivity or prejudice. If this happens (even if in your heart, mind, and soul, you know they are lying!), you should respond by saying

Do not get into an argument with parents about whether or not their child presents the negative behavior only at school, not at home.

that what they've told you is surprising and perplexing. Nevertheless, maintain that the behavior is problematic in the classroom and on the playground and that it bodes poorly for their child's academic and social success. Do not get into an argument about whether or not it really does or doesn't happen at home or what happened in previous classes. If you know that the behavior occurred in previous classes in your school, you may mention that you have confirmed as much with the child's previous teacher. But if the parents remain in denial, then an argument will not be productive. Move on to the next issue.

Reaffirm and Then Seek Interpretations

Reaffirm the data and observations you have listed. Then ask the parents, "What do you think this is about?" Keep your opinions to yourself at this point. Asking the parents to present what they think is going on with the child gives you insight into their experiences. In addition, this often gives you the opportunity to discover for the first time issues that the parents may have been holding back, which could be relevant to their child's behavior.

Children with difficult behaviors or with significant challenges to their functioning have usually experienced a series of failures in academic and other community experiences. Parents of such children will sometimes try to move them into a new situation, with the hope that the issue will not present itself again. They hope (against experience and reality) that this time the child will do fine just because it is a different situation. They are hopeful that it was the previous environment and teachers that caused the child's challenging behavior. This way, they can avoid considering that there may be something about their child that makes him or her ill-equipped to handle community expectations. Parents will often keep the negative previous experiences and the negative behavior issues of their child a secret from the new teacher and school. However, when presented with the list of negative behaviors (behaviors they have experienced before), then and only then will some of them confess what they know to be true.

Interventions: From Hope to Collaboration

A kindergarten teacher had in her class a difficult child with significant attention, hyperactivity, and distractibility issues. She approached the parents with a list of her observations of the child's behavior. The parents listened quietly, with somber expressions. When the teacher asked them what they thought their daughter's issues might be about, the mother burst into tears. She told the teacher that their daughter was adopted and her biological mother was a crack (cocaine) addict. Their daughter had prenatal exposure to the crack in her biological mother's system. She had always had challenges since they had adopted her as an infant, but they had been hoping that she would outgrow these challenges and do well in kindergarten. They did not want her to be labeled as a "crack baby" by informing teachers and administrators of her biological mother's past. Their hope was their intervention, but it was not successful.

Once the parents communicated the new information, however, they were able to form an alliance with the teacher to best serve the girl. A series of interventions came out of the collaboration. As in this case, parents initially hold secrets that they are afraid will prejudice a teacher against their children, and they will share information only if asked specifically. If you have the insight to ask specific questions, parents will normally give you the information you seek (if they have it) and will also develop a deeper respect for you and a sense of alliance. This benefits future relationships and collaboration to serve the children.

Growing Out of It

In the previous example, Shelley's parents also acknowledged that they had observed her atypical behaviors at home. Unfortunately, they were unable or were unwilling to speculate as to what her issues stemmed from. They made vague reference to Shelley "growing out of it." As teachers with experience with tens or hundreds of children, there are many behaviors you recognize that children may grow out of. However, there are also some issues for which growth and maturity and the development process are not sufficient to overcome. When parents do not recognize this, you have to decide whether it is useful to share your interpretations about what may be going on with their child. With regard to Shelley, the preschool director acknowledged that although he didn't know specifically what was going on with Shelley, he knew that it was either unusual or harmful to her academic success. He therefore recommended that they seek a professional diagnosis for their daughter.

Diagnoses and Recommendations Outside the Teacher's Realm

Teachers learn about related issues in related fields of work with continuing education and staff development training. Such training enhances your work and gives you insight as to where your work overlaps with other fields. That, however, does not make you an expert to perform professional diagnosis outside of your realm or scope of practice. As a psychotherapist, I take care not to make diagnoses that are in the realm of a psychiatrist. I may indicate to clients that their depth of anxiety and/or depression may be so great that they may consider talking to a psychiatrist to find out whether psychotropic medication may serve them. I am experienced as an educator from early childhood centers through elementary school and high school, so it is both within my scope of competence and my scope of practice to consult about behavioral issues in educational settings. However, even though I have knowledge and experience as a clinician with students with emotional disturbances and learning disabilities, I am not a speech and language specialist or a neurologist. I am familiar with the autistic spectrum, but I am not an expert or specialist on developing such children's social skills.

As a responsible educator, you need to become versed in the related professional areas that may affect a child's ability to be successful in school. As you develop this expertise and knowledge, you also need to know the limits of it. Your professional responsibility is to recognize that something is amiss. You need to determine whether there is something "off" and, if so, refer the child to the appropriate professional with the specific expertise to make an appropriate diagnosis and perhaps intervention. This professional may also be able to give you recommendations that will improve your work with the child in the classroom.

Pushing Parents

Shelley's parents listened to the preschool director's recommendation that they seek additional professional advice. They said they would think about it. A week later, the director asked them what they had done about it. They said that they were still thinking about it. Another week passed, and he asked them again. They said they were looking at some possibilities. When asked to specify, they made some vague references about getting some referrals from friends. Teachers and therapists tend to be very intuitive and socially adept individuals. They can read the nuances of nonverbal communication quite well—and the nonverbal communication from these parents was for the director to leave them alone!

As the teacher, your professional responsibility is not to make parents happy or to make them like you, but to advocate in the best interests of the children in your class.

They were in denial. Since they wanted to avoid dealing with Shelley's issues, they did not appreciate his continued questions. As he had clearly picked up this cue, the director's personal reaction as a socially adept individual could have been to let it go. However, his professional responsibility as an educator was to continue to press this issue. Although parents have the final say in what they do with their children, parental irresponsibility does not excuse or condone professional irresponsibility.

The Professional Mirror

Periodically, the director continued to ask Shelley's parents about which professional resource they had chosen to help Shelley, and he continued to tell them about her behavior in school. If her behavior had been compromising the well-being of the other children, the director would have had to require her leave the school, but because her behavior was not harmful to others, she remained. Shelley's parents continued to make vague comments about getting her some help, and the director continued to make himself professionally obnoxious! Eventually, Shelley's parents could no longer tolerate the mirror he had placed in front of them, and so they withdrew her from the preschool.

About 6 years later, the director received a call from Shelley's father, who was in another state. He said, "Shelley's school district has just diagnosed her with autism. Since you were the first one to notice differences in Shelley, could you please write a report about what you observed when she was 4 years old?" Though the director was pleased that Shelley would finally receive the services she needed and he had referred her to, he was furious that she hadn't received early intervention, which could have made a huge difference.

It's not easy, but teachers must communicate their expertise and experience to parents in professional and appropriate ways—and be stubborn about it! Children leave your classroom after a year, but your stubborn gift of honesty may serve to enable other professionals to have the impact that you cannot have at the time. Shelley had actually had two prior early childhood professionals who knew her who should have expressed concerns to the parents, prior to the preschool director. If your aim is to help the children in your class realize a life with promise and positivity, you need to be professional and tenacious in communicating to their parents. Though you may make some waves, you will keep your integrity as an educator, as a professional, and as an advocate for children.

Chapter Highlights

- For a happy child who misbehaves, the areas to examine include developmental issues, specific situations, physical condition, disruptions in routines, temperamental traits, and the dynamics of the social situations.
- Anger is often secondary to a more vulnerable emotion. Males, in particular, are encouraged to use anger to handle or hide more vulnerable emotions.
- Children may need significant help in learning how to express anger appropriately.
- Teachers and other adults may offer certain children reparative relationships that help heal emotional traumas.
- Children who are unappreciated, ignored, and devalued may be depressed but still able to function relatively well.
- Simply showing interest in children's feelings validates them.
- Fear is specific and, as such, may be relatively easy to eliminate through experience and adult support.
- Anxiety results from consistent overall unpredictability and negative experiences. It is nonspecific and ambiguous and harder to eliminate. It can derive from family instability and/or classroom instability.
- Anxiety is mitigated by stability and predictability.
- Children who do not see models of grieving, who are not supported in their grieving, or who are discouraged from grieving may end up holding pain and loss to their detriment.
- Teachers need to support children in their grieving processes.
- Recognizing that a child is exhibiting behavior or characteristics that are outside the range of what is considered "normal" requires the teacher to recommend that parents seek the advice of a more specialized professional.
- When communicating concerns to parents, teachers can try a three-point process: (1) presenting data/observations, (2) soliciting and then offering interpretations, and (3) discussing and recommending interventions.
- Despite parental resistance or denial, teachers, as professionals, must share and discuss their observations with parents.

Conclusion

Now What?

I read the book, but I still have

- an anxious boy;
- a bright but off-track girl;
- a sweet kid who hits;
- an active child who is getting worse;
- a child who doesn't care anymore;
- a student who does something wrong, knowing he'll be caught;
- doubts about timeout;
- the kid who can't keep his hands to himself;
- a sense that something is not right.

Are you still asking "What should I do when . . . ?" There is a better question to begin with. You are faced with a problematic child, a challenging situation, something confusing, or something not working well. What should you do? The first thing you should do is ask a lot of questions. Another appropriate form of the first question to ask is "What are all the questions I need to ask to get the information needed to help this child?" The series of questions in Chapter 14 about anger, sadness, anxiety or fear, loss or pain, or needing special services is just a beginning. Ask many questions as you reflect on yourself and as you conduct classroom and playground observations. Ask questions about the child, the circumstances, the community, and yourself.

Asking Questions

Here's a list of questions to ask yourself, to help get started:

- What have I observed?
- What have I experienced with this child?
- What have I experienced with other children?
- What is the feedback from other observers?
- What is similar to other children or situations? What is different?

- What do I expect? Why do I expect that? Why not expect something else?
- What are my assumptions? Are they accurate assumptions? Why or why not?

- What has worked before for this child? Why?
- What hasn't worked? Why not?
- What has worked or not worked for other children? Why or why not?

- How is the behavior or functioning developmentally appropriate or inappropriate?
- Is there an issue about limited resources or access? If so, what is the effect?

- When does this problematic behavior occur? Why then rather than at another time?
- What physical condition (tired or hungry, for example) is the child in when the behavior occurs? What happens if that is addressed?
- What physical condition (tired or hungry, for example) am I in when the behavior occurs? What happens if that is addressed?

- Is there anything different or new going on in the classroom, at home, or anywhere else in the child's life? In my life?
- How does the child respond to change? How well do I handle change?
- How well does the child handle transitions? How do I present transitions?

- What aspects of the child's personality are potentially problematic?

- What aspects of my personality are potentially problematic?
- How does my personality mesh with the child's personality?

- What is the level of stimulation during problematic situations? Noise level? Activity level?
- Which stimulation levels work better for the child? For me?
- At what point does the child get overstimulated? At what point do I get overstimulated?
- How does the child respond to being overstimulated? How do I respond?

- What is the communication style of the child? How is it similar or different from my communication style?
- How explicit, as opposed to implicit, is the communication? How well does it work?
- How much verbal versus nonverbal communication do the child and I use during our interactions?
- How much verbal versus nonverbal communication is used among the other children and the problematic child?

- How do the child's responses help or further harm the problematic behavior?
- How do my responses help or further harm the problematic behavior?

- How is my classroom similar or different from the child's previous classroom?
- How is my classroom similar or different from the child's household?
- How do class expectations and rules match or mismatch with prior classroom and/or household expectations?

- Are there cross-cultural differences that affect expectations and behavior? If so, what are they, and what effects do they have?
- How can I address cross-cultural issues with children? With parents?

- How stable is the classroom environment? Physically? Emotionally? Socially? Intellectually?
- How does that stability (or instability) affect the child's attitude, mood, and behavior?
- How does that stability (or instability) affect my attitude, mood, and behavior?

- What are other possible stresses or influences on the child, classroom, or home? How do they affect attitude, mood, and behavior?
- What are other possible stresses or influences on me personally or professionally (administration or standards, for example)? How do they affect my attitude, mood, and behavior?
- What is the classroom atmosphere (or culture)? How does it fit into the problematic child's experience? How does it support or stress the child?

- To what extent (and how) are parents or other caregivers involved in the child's academic process?
- How well am I able to work with the child's parents?
- How informed and educated are parents/caregivers regarding the child's needs and performance? What can I do to support or advance that?
- How healthy or functional is the family support system? What can I do to support or enhance that?

- How do the other children positively or negatively affect the problematic child?
- How does the problematic child positively or negatively affect the other children?
- Is there a particular child or are there particular children with whom the problematic child has more conflicts? Why? What is the nature of provocation in either direction?

- How healthy or functional is the school support system? What can I do to support or enhance that?
- What issues does the child present that are within my *scope of competence* (by training, education, or experience)? What issues are not (for example, a child who may present a developmental delay)?
- What issues does the child present that are within my *scope of practice* (by the legal definitions and limitations of your teaching credential)? What issues are not? (For example, a teacher should never tell parents to put their child on medication for attention deficit disorder. That would be making not only a medical diagnosis but also a medical recommendation. Teachers are not doctors or therapists.)
- What other opinions, experience, resources, consultation, or support (within the school, other professionals, or community) can be accessed to support the child? How can I help access those resources on behalf of the child and family?

And, finally, this is the last questions to ask: "What *other* questions do I need to ask? Is there anything else?"

From Observations to Results

By gathering all of the relevant information you can, the process to help and discipline children can begin. Your **OBSERVATIONS** of what may be going on will suggest **THEORIES** to be explored. These may or may not be your "favorite" theories. If evidence exists that there has been inconsistency in setting and following through on clear boundaries, you may follow through with **STRATEGIES** to create consistency and clarity. If the child seems to be unmotivated, to create motivation (the strategy), you may choose the specific **INTERVENTION** of a behavior incentive plan. If you realize that a particular situation (inconsistency in being brought to school on time) has led to a problem (child anxiety that leads to acting-out behavior), then you may want to set stricter boundaries (regarding parent timeliness). However, if you won't let yourself do that because your **STYLE** is to avoid confrontation, you will encounter difficulty in making progress. If your style allows you to follow through, you can achieve two types of **RESULTS:**

1. *Boundaries* will be set, and the child will be in class. The child will feel secure that he or she won't miss out by being late.

2. By being in class, the child can experience *growth and change*, academically and socially.

OBSERVATIONS → THEORIES → STRATEGIES →
INTERVENTIONS → STYLE → RESULTS

This book suggested areas to investigate when observing and understanding why children misbehave. Questions were introduced and theories discussed. Timeout theory and behavior incentive theory led to major discussions of subsequent strategies and specific interventions. Inhibitions and misunderstandings were explored to show how a teacher's style can sabotage good interventions derived from sound theories. The discussion on boundaries clarified the need to assert the first set of results and established how boundaries set the foundation for the second set of results: growth and change. In addition, a series of intuitive and subjective questions prompted adults to analyze their observations and consider possible underlying emotional issues. Did this make sense? I hope so. But you may still want a specific answer to your question "What do I do when . . . ?"

Be a Teaching Artist

If this book were an instructional manual about painting and I were a painting teacher, I'd remind you about the book's and my limits. I could teach you how to mix colors to get the right color red. But only you know when it is the right shade and intensity of red. I could teach you how to use different brushes and different techniques to get certain effects on the canvas. But as you bring the brush to the canvas, you must choose how deep or broad of a stroke will create the image you want. The techniques, skills, and craft of painting can be taught. However, it takes a special person with special qualities to be an artist.

Education, experience, and training will enhance the analytical skills, teaching techniques, and conceptual and curricular sophistication of a teacher. A conscientious professional will strive to develop all of these things. This book seeks to aid in that process. However, in the moment that counts, with the challenge confronting you, with a child sitting before you, you are not just a technician or craftsperson. You must be an artist. Teaching and parenting will always be more than technique, theory, strategy, skills, and craft. It will be about art. What do people add to technique, theory, strategy, skills, and craft in order to become great artists? They add great commitment and great passion. This book can help with your craft to be a competent teacher, but it will not provide or replace the commitment and passion that are necessary for you to be great.

Children are our greatest artist compositions. Often our most difficult challenges, our most problematic children, become our greatest accomplishments. Your love and commitment to your children will keep you asking questions. They will keep you exploring and learning. They will help you make continued effort when you are feeling unfulfilled, unsupported, unrewarded, unappreciated, and frustrated. You will continue to strive to meet the needs of the most difficult children so that they can become children who used to have problems. Commitment and passion will turn you into the great artist, great teacher, or great parent you want to be or that children need you to be. Hone your craft, broaden your knowledge, deepen your sophistication, but above all, be great!

References

Abraham, H. D., & Fava, M. (1999). Order of onset of substance abuse and depression in a sample of depressed outpatients. *Comprehensive Psychiatry, 40*(1), 44–50.

Allard, H. (1985). *Miss Nelson is missing.* Boston: Houghton Mifflin.

Barkley, R. A., Edwards, G., Laneri, M., Fletcher, K., & Metevia, L. (2001). Executive functioning, temporal discounting, and sense of time in adolescents with attention deficit hyperactivity disorder (ADHD) and oppositional defiant disorder (ODD). *Journal of Abnormal Child Psychology, 29,* 541–546.

Barkley, R. A., Koplowitz, S., Anderson, T., & McMurray, M. B. (1997). Sense of time in children with ADHD: Effects of duration, distraction, and stimulant medication. *Journal of the International Neuropsychological Society, 3,* 359–369.

Barnet, A. B., & Barnet, R. J. (1998). *The youngest minds: Parenting and genes in the development of intellect and emotion.* New York: Simon & Schuster.

Brandt, R. (1995). Punished by rewards? A conversation with Alfie Kohn. *Educational Leadership, 53*(1), 13–15.

Canter, L. (1992). *Lee Canter's assertive discipline.* Santa Monica, CA: Canter & Associates.

Carroll, R. T. (2005). Becoming a critical thinker. *The skeptic's dictionary.* Retrieved January 22, 2006, from skepdic.com/science

Collins, M. (1992). *Ordinary children, extraordinary teachers.* Charleston, VA: Hampton Road.

Curwin, R. L., & Mendler, A. N. (1997). *As tough as necessary: Countering violence, aggression, and hostility in our schools.* Alexandria, VA: Association for Supervision and Curriculum Development.

Dunn, L. J. (2004). *Nonverbal communication: Information conveyed through the use of body language.* St. Joseph, MO: National Undergraduate Research Clearinghouse, Division of Psychology, Missouri Western State University.

Elkind, D. (1999). A context for learning: Educating young children in math, science, and technology. *Dialogue on early childhood science, mathematics, and technology education* (Project 2061, American Association for the

Advancement of Science). Washington, DC: American Association for the Advancement of Science.

Fay, J., & Funk, D. (1995). *Teaching with love and logic: Taking control of the classroom.* Golden, CO: Love and Logic Press.

Fitzsimmons, M. K. (1998, November). *Violence and aggression in children and youth.* Arlington VA: Council for Exceptional Children. (ERIC Clearinghouse on Disabilities and Gifted Education, EC Digest #E572)

Glasser, W. (1998). *Choice theory: A new psychology of personal freedom.* New York: HarperCollins.

Gootman, M. (2001). *The caring teacher's guide to discipline.* Thousand Oaks, CA: Corwin Press.

Grant, B. F. (2004, August). Substance use and mood and anxiety disorders among the most prevalent psychiatric disorders. *Archives of General Psychiatry, 61,* 807–816.

Jensen, E. (1997). *Completing the puzzle: The brain-compatible approach to learning.* Del Mar, CA: The Brain Store.

Kohn, A. (1992). *The brighter side of human nature: Altruism and empathy in everyday life.* New York: Basic.

Kohn, A. (1993). *Punished by rewards.* Boston: Houghton Mifflin.

Kohn, A. (2000a, May). Hooked on praise. *Parents Magazine, 1.*

Kohn, A. (2000b). Raising children who care. *NAMTA Journal, 25*(2), 185 206.

Kohn, A. (2001, September). Five reasons to stop saying "Good job!" *Young Children, 1.*

Kübler-Ross, E. (1969). *On death and dying.* New York: Simon & Schuster.

Marshall, M. (1998). Rethinking our thinking on discipline: Empower— rather than overpower. *Education Week, XVII*(37), 32.

Marshall, M. (2003, March). Discipline without stress, punishment, or rewards. *Phi Delta Kappan, Professional Journal for Education.* Retrieved August 8, 2005, from http://www.pdkintl.org/kappan/k0403mar.htm

Marshall, M., & Weisner, K. (2004). Using a discipline system to promote learning. *Phi Delta Kappan, Professional Journal for Education 85*(7), 498–507.

McGregor, D. (1960). *The human side of enterprise.* New York: McGraw-Hill.

Morrish, R. (n.d.). *What is real discipline?* Retrieved August 8, 2005, from http://www.realdiscipline.com/index.html

National PTA. (1993). *Discipline: A parents' guide.* Chicago: Author.

O'Connell, T. (2005, April 1). Cannabis use in adolescence: Self-medication for anxiety. *O'Shaughnessy's* (Journal of the California Cannabis Research Medical Group).

Payne, R. (1996). *A framework for understanding poverty.* Highlands, TX: aha! Process, Inc., Audio Journal of Education.

Pruitt, C. T., & Lebo, J. (1998). *Big bucks: A creative discipline system.* Gainesville, FL: Maupin House.

Selman, R. (1973, March). *A structural analysis of the ability to take another's social perspective: Stages in the development of role-taking ability.* Paper presented at the meeting of the Society of Research in Child Development, Philadelphia, PA.

Skinner, B. F. (1938). *The behavior of organisms: An experimental analysis.* New York: Appleton-Century.

Smith, R. (2004). *Conscious classroom management: Unlocking the secrets of great teaching.* San Rafael, CA: Conscious Teaching Publications.

Sylwester, R. (2000). Unconscious emotions, conscious feelings, curricular challenges. *Educational Leadership, 58*(3), 20–24.

Sylwester, R. (2003). *A biological brain in a cultural classroom.* Thousand Oaks, CA: Corwin Press.

Tileston, D. W. (2004). *What every teacher should know about classroom management and discipline.* Thousand Oaks, CA: Corwin Press.

Turiel, E. (1998). *The development of morality. Handbook of child psychology* (Vol. 3, 5th ed., pp. 863–932). New York: Wiley.

Wong, H. (1991). *The first days of school: How to be an effective teacher.* Mountain View, CA: Harry K. Wong Publications. Retrieved January 22, 2006, from http://www.glavac.com/harrywong.htm

Index

**CORWIN
PRESS**

The Corwin Press logo—a raven striding across an open book—represents the union of courage and learning. Corwin Press is committed to improving education for all learners by publishing books and other professional development resources for those serving the field of PreK–12 education. By providing practical, hands-on materials, Corwin Press continues to carry out the promise of its motto: **"Helping Educators Do Their Work Better."**